Each &
Every Child

Teaching Preschool with an Equity Lens

Susan Friedman &
Alissa Mwenelupembe

EDITORS

National Association for the Education of Young Children

Washington, DC

National Association for the Education of Young Children

NAEYC.org

NAEYC Books

Senior Director, Publishing
& Professional Learning
Susan Friedman

Senior Editor
Holly Bohart

Editor
Rossella Procopio

Senior Creative
Design Manager
Henrique J. Siblesz

Senior Creative
Design Specialist
Gillian Frank

Senior Creative
Design Specialist
Charity Coleman

Publishing Business
Operations Manager
Francine Markowitz

Through its publications program, the National Association for the Education of Young Children (NAEYC) provides a forum for discussion of major issues and ideas in the early childhood field, with the hope of provoking thought and promoting professional growth. The views expressed or implied in this book are not necessarily those of the Association.

The following chapters were previously published in the specified issues of *Teaching Young Children*: August/September 2017—Chapter 6; December 2017/January 2018—Chapter 8; December 2018/January 2019—Chapters 10, 15, 18, and 20; February/March 2019—Chapters 4, 12, and 16; April/May 2019—Chapters 2, 9, 13, and 21; August/September 2019—Chapters 14 and 17; and December 2019/January 2020—Chapters 3 and 7.

Chapter 1 is adapted from L. Derman-Sparks & J.O. Edwards with C.M. Goins, *Anti-Bias Education for Young Children and Ourselves,* 2nd ed. (Washington, DC: NAEYC, 2020).

Chapter 2 is adapted from C.L. Price & E.A. Steed, "Culturally Responsive Strategies to Support Young Children with Challenging Behavior," *Young Children* 71, no. 5 (2016): 36–43.

Chapter 5 is adapted from B. Hassinger-Das, K. Hirsh-Pasek, & R.M. Golinkoff, "The Case of Brain Science and Guided Play: A Developing Story," *Young Children* 72, no. 2 (2017): 45–50.

Chapter 10 is adapted from S.B. Wanless & P.A. Crawford, "Reading Your Way to a Culturally Responsive Classroom," *Young Children* 71, no. 2 (2016): 8–15.

Permissions

NAEYC accepts requests for limited use of our copyrighted material. For permission to reprint, adapt, translate, or otherwise reuse and repurpose content from this publication, review our guidelines at NAEYC.org/resources/permissions.

Purchasers of *Each and Every Child: Teaching Preschool with an Equity Lens* are permitted to photocopy "Fun, Easy Ways to Play with Math at Home: A Resource for Families" on pages 124–125 for distribution to families or for other educational or training purposes only. Photocopies may be made only from an original book.

Chapter 14 is adapted, with permission, from Education Development Center (EDC), *Supporting Emergent Bilingual Children in Early Learning: Promising Practices and Checklist* (Waltham, MA: EDC, 2019), www.edc.org/sites/default/files/uploads/Supporting-Emergent-Bilingual-Children_English.pdf.

Chapter 20 is adapted, with permission, from EDC, *Games for Young Mathematicians* (Waltham, MA: EDC, 2019), www.ym.edc.org.

Chapter 22 is adapted, with permission, from J. Solomon, "Understanding Children as Community Leaders," in *Innovations in Early Education: The International Reggio Emilia Exchange* 24, no. 3 (2017): 48–62.

Cover Photo Credits
Copyright © Getty Images

Library of Congress Control Number: 2019950265

ISBN: 978-1-938113-61-1

Item 1144

Contents

Introduction

As a teacher of young children, you have the power to change children's lives through what you do every day. The attention you give to the learning environment you create and your willingness to reflect on and address your own beliefs and teaching practices matter enormously. NAEYC's position statement "Advancing Equity in Early Childhood Education" says that

1. All children have the right to equitable learning opportunities that help them achieve their full potential.
2. All early childhood educators have a professional obligation to advance equity.
3. Early childhood educators need support to fulfill their mission.

Working to achieve equity in early childhood education settings involves a wide range of small- and large-scale actions and commitments by the field as a whole and by individual educators, from recognizing and understanding how structural inequities have limited children's learning opportunities to being responsive to each child's specific learning needs within the context of his culture, family structure, language, racial identity, gender, abilities and disabilities, religious beliefs, and economic class.

Early childhood educators play a critical role in the development of young children and must work to

- Create a caring, equitable community of engaged learners
- Establish two-way relationships that respect families' expertise
- Ensure that all children are building foundational knowledge, vocabulary, and skills
- Use a range of teaching approaches to provide all children with the learning supports they need
- Observe, document, and assess children's learning and development, acknowledging the potential for implicit bias based on their own experiences
- Advocate on behalf of young children, families, and the early childhood profession

Being an early childhood education professional also means a commitment to self-reflection, a willingness to respectfully listen to others' perspectives without interruption or defensiveness, and continuous learning to improve practice.

The information that follows explaining what equity is and why it is important is adapted from a larger, more comprehensive supplement to the position statement on equity developed by NAEYC.

Equity Is Not the Same as Equality

While both concepts are important, *equity* and *equality* are not the same. *Equity* means all children and families get the supports they need to develop their full intellectual, social, emotional, linguistic, and physical potential. For teachers, equity builds on the widespread practice of meeting children where they are developmentally and extends the concept to consider all the unique strengths each child has and to intentionally ask how to build upon those strengths with activities, materials, and environments to maximize learning. Equitable teaching often includes working with families to create connections that extend and enrich learning.

Giving equal treatment to individuals at unequal starting points is inequitable. Instead of equal treatment, NAEYC aims for equal opportunity. This requires considering individuals' and groups' starting points, then distributing resources equitably (not equally) to meet their needs. Attempting to achieve equality of opportunity without considering historic and present inequities is ineffective, unjust, and unfair. For teachers, it is important to keep in mind that what a child currently knows and is able to do is largely a reflection of the opportunities that child has had to learn—and not necessarily a good indicator of what the child is capable of learning.

Why Equity Matters in Early Childhood

Early childhood education settings—including centers, family child care homes, and schools—are often children's first communities outside the home. These settings offer important contexts for children's learning. They should be environments in which children learn that they are valued by others, learn how to treat others with fairness and respect, and learn how to embrace human differences rather than ignore or fear them.

Why Now

The research base regarding the impact of implicit bias in early childhood settings is growing. Teachers of young children—like all people—are not immune to such bias. Even among teachers who do not believe they hold any explicit biases, implicit biases may lead to different expectations and treatment of children based on their race, gender, ability and disability, family structure and composition, body type, physical appearance, language, or social and economic status.

Implicit biases also result in differential judgments of children's play, aggressiveness, compliance, initiative, and abilities. These biases limit children's opportunities to reach their potential. They are associated with lower rates of achievement and assignment to gifted services and disproportionately higher rates of suspension and expulsion, beginning in preschool, for African American and Latino children, especially boys.

There is growing awareness of the extraordinary ability that all young children have to learn, including learning multiple languages, engaging in critical thinking, and understanding many complex topics and ideas that researchers used to believe were too advanced for young children.

About this Book

Advancing equity can seem overwhelming when you're an educator working every day with young children. You may have many different family languages within your classroom. Your background and experiences may be very different from that of children you teach. How do you adapt your teaching to give children the specific learning supports they each need?

Promoting equity in your classroom *is* within your reach, and this book will give you some of the tools you need. It focuses on what equity work can look like for teachers working with children ages 3 through 5 on a day-to-day basis in the classroom. Each contribution featured in this volume has been carefully selected because it embodies key messages from NAEYC's position statement on equity and offers inspiration for how you can implement many of those important ideas. You will find strategies and tips for how you can support the learning and development of each and every child in your classroom through intentional play opportunities and guided instructional supports. The chapters address a range of topics, including race, language, family structure, and ability, for you to explore and consider as you develop a strengths-based approach to teaching. The questions included at the beginning of each of the book's six sections invite you to evaluate how you might embed these ideas in your classroom, to reflect on the potential effects of implicit bias, and to think more deeply about how you can support diverse children and families.

The full scope of equity work cannot be addressed in a single book, and it is important to note that this collection does not cover the full breadth of topics discussed within the position statement. Consider this just one resource on your journey to teaching with an equity lens. NAEYC's position statement on equity, along with many more tools and resources, can be found at NAEYC.org/equity.

Uphold the unique value and dignity of each child and family. Ensure that all children see themselves and their daily experiences, as well as the daily lives of others within and beyond their community, positively reflected in the design and implementation of pedagogy, curriculum, learning environment, interactions, and materials. Celebrate diversity by acknowledging similarities and differences and provide perspectives that recognize beauty and value across differences.

Recognize each child's unique strengths and support the full inclusion of all children— given differences in culture, family structure, language, racial identity, gender, abilities and disabilities, religious beliefs, or economic class. Help children get to know, recognize, and support one another as valued members of the community. Take care that no one feels bullied, invisible, or unnoticed.

PART 1

Nurturing Your Own Empathy and Understanding Behavior

What would the world be like if everyone practiced empathy and made a conscious effort to understand the perspectives of others? Now think about the sort of education that is required for such a world. To learn empathy, children need to be surrounded by it and see it at the heart of every interaction they have with adults they trust as well as other children. As a teacher, you play a huge role in supporting and instilling this value by creating a warm, inclusive learning environment that respects and celebrates different experiences, cultures, and backgrounds.

Part of developing and nurturing empathy is recognizing that everyone has their own cultural lens that guides their behaviors and informs their interactions with and expectations of others. When a child's behavior in the classroom deviates from a teacher's expectations, the teacher might look for tools to change or manage that behavior. But sometimes children's behaviors are tied to cultural norms and expectations that are simply different from your own. Looking at the whole child and considering how that child's culture and experiences shape his behavior are key to being a culturally responsive teacher who knows how to effectively support each child in your classroom. As you read the chapters in this section, think about the children you work with, especially those who you sometimes find challenging. What might you not know about each child? How might you go deeper in your relationship with each child's family to learn more?

Read and Reflect

As you read the chapters in this section, consider and evaluate your own classroom practices using these reflection questions.

1. Everyone has biases (implicit and explicit) that contribute to their interactions, their understanding of situations, and the messages sent to children. Think of a time when your biases may have affected your perception of a child's behavior. What was your initial perception? What did you later consider, and how did that consideration change your initial perception?

2. Take a moment to reflect on the circle time vignette in Chapter 1 (page 9). Try filming part of your day as those teachers did and watch the recording with a colleague. What does the video recording reveal that you didn't notice in the heat of the moment? How can you make sure your own biases aren't leading to increased discipline for one group of children?

3. Research shows that teachers tend to be less empathetic with children who have different ethnic and cultural backgrounds from their own. Select two of the suggested practices outlined in Chapter 2 (page 15) to improve upon in your own work with children. Which practices did you choose to focus on and why? What will you do differently?

4. Chapter 3 (page 19) discusses how each person's upbringing influences her work with young children. Take a moment and reflect on your childhood. What values did your family have? How might those values influence your own values today?

5. For young children, representation matters. Why do you think it is important for the children you teach to see themselves represented in their classroom? How does this connect to empathy and showing children you see and care about them? What changes could you make to the books on your shelf or the images on your walls to make them more representative? Brainstorm a list of ways you can add representations of diversity to your classroom.

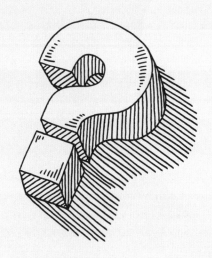

CHAPTER 1

Examining Teacher Bias

Louise Derman-Sparks and Julie Olsen Edwards, with Catherine M. Goins

Early childhood educators are committed to the principle that every child deserves to develop to her fullest potential. At the same time, the world is not yet a place where all children have equal opportunity to become all they can be. Beyond an individual teacher's hopes, beliefs, and actions is a society that has built advantage and disadvantage into its institutions and systems. These dynamics of advantage and disadvantage are deeply rooted in history. They continue to shape the degree of access children have to education, health care, and security—the services necessary for children's healthy development. They also generate messages and actions that directly and indirectly reinforce harmful ideas and stereotyping and that undermine children's sense of worth, especially when they come from someone as significant as a teacher.

This chapter is adapted from Derman-Sparks & Edwards with Goins 2020.

Anti-bias education is an optimistic commitment to supporting all children in a highly diverse and yet still inequitable world. It is founded on the understanding that as well as having individual temperaments and personalities, children have social group identities based on the families who raise them and the way society views who they are. These identities are both externally applied by the world around them and internally constructed within the child.

Anti-bias educators actively foster children feeling good about all aspects of themselves, including their social identities, without developing a false sense of superiority based on who they are. These teachers recognize that children are injured when they receive messages about themselves that say they are not fully capable and intelligent or when adults become silent in the face of children teasing or rejecting others because of their identities. But despite their best intentions, many teachers carry unconscious biases that impact their behavior and curriculums in ways that are hurtful to children's identity development.

Biases Are Everywhere

Biases are beliefs that affect how individuals think, feel, and act toward others. They lead to acts of individual prejudice and discrimination. Starting in childhood, everyone absorbs and internalizes biases from larger societal attitudes (Bian, Leslie, & Cimpian 2017; Brown et al. 2017). As adults, early childhood teachers bring these ideas consciously or unconsciously into their work (Yates & Marcelo 2014). This is why it is essential for teachers to understand how biases work—and uncover and get rid of their own.

Despite the values individual teachers may hold, such biases influence what happens in early childhood education programs. For example, some teachers may assume families are not interested in their preschoolers' education because they often miss family conferences, meetings, or other events, without considering that many families are unable to attend due to such factors as the cost of babysitting, lack of available transportation, or inflexible work hours, or that discussions with their child's teacher are not in the family's language.

Biases Are Explicit *and* Implicit

Sometimes a person's bias is obvious, or *explicit*. Explicit biases are undisguised statements. They are attitudes and beliefs about a group of people that are applied to all individuals in the group. Most early childhood educators are sensitive to explicit bias and, for the most part, work hard to avoid and address such behavior. Still, the field is plagued by some explicit biases, such as the belief that children in some racial groups are genetically more intelligent than other racial groups, that boys are inherently more destructive than girls, and that adopted children carry lifelong emotional damage.

In other cases, a person's actions reflect bias that is not so obvious—even to the person acting on it. This is *implicit* bias. Implicit biases are "attitudes or stereotypes that affect our understanding, actions, and decisions in an unconscious manner" (Kirwan Institute 2015). Individuals may not be aware that they have these biases or that they act or fail to act because of their implicit biases. For example, in our experience, White teachers who say that they are "color blind" (i.e., are not aware of racial or ethnic differences because "children are children") tend to have classrooms in which White, urban, middle-class children are represented in the learning environment and curriculum, while children of other backgrounds are not. Regardless of the teacher's conscious intentions, this kind of classroom sends all children the message that the "universal" child is White, middle class, urban, able-bodied, from a two-parent family, and therefore the one who matters. Children who do not fit in those categories are "less than," "different," "exotic," not "regular." These teachers may not express *explicit* biases that being White or middle class is better, but their implicit bias about what the "universal child" looks like turns into racial bias in practice and reinforces the societal inequities and injuries the child meets outside the classroom.

> Teachers of young children—like all people—are not immune to such bias. Even among teachers who do not believe they hold any explicit biases, implicit biases are associated with differential judgments about and treatment of children by race, gender, ability, body type, physical appearance, and social, economic, and language status—all of which limit children's opportunities to reach their potential. Implicit biases also result in differential judgments of children's play, aggressiveness, compliance, initiative, and abilities. (NAEYC 2019, 15)

Even when teachers intend to foster all children's growth and are unaware of the influence of specific biases, damage is done when early childhood programs and teacher interactions with children reflect the implicit and explicit biases of the larger society.

Implicit Biases Impact Teachers' Behavior and Children's Well-Being

Consider how young girls often receive feedback about the way they look and the way they are dressed rather than about their abilities, while boys are praised for their efforts and accomplishments. Bit by bit, many girls become convinced that their value rests mainly on their appearance, a belief that becomes increasingly toxic for teens and young adults and tends to shadow the adult lives of many women (OWH 2019).

Another deeply hurtful—and well researched—example of implicit biases influencing teacher behavior is documentation that African American boys are disproportionately suspended from preschool programs for behavioral issues. Oscar Barbarin was one of the first to look at this disturbing reality (Barbarin & Crawford 2006). Several years later, the US Department of Education's Office for Civil Rights (OCR) reported that African American children "represent 18 percent of preschool enrollment, but 48 percent of preschool children receiving more than one out-of-school suspension" (2014, 1). And although the teachers and directors who suspend these boys may not be acting with the conscious intent of being racist, their unexamined implicit bias results in racism.

Here is an example of a preservice teacher in one of Julie's college classes facing an important learning moment concerning how implicit bias resulted in an incorrect and unfair interpretation of children's behavior:

A preservice teacher was recorded doing circle time. The activity had fallen apart, with children getting up, running away, and refusing to participate. That evening the class discussed what happened. The student teacher complained about the disruptive behavior of two African American boys who had "ruined" the circle. Then the instructor played the video recording. Everyone was shocked to see that the real disruption had come from two White boys, that one of the African American boys had joined in later, and that the second boy had been almost entirely a bystander. "But I remembered it as Alec and William!" the student teacher said in tears. "How could I have been so wrong?"

We All Learn Explicit and Implicit Biases

One of the great gifts of teaching is the way it requires you to keep growing. Uncovering and eliminating prejudicial ideas and behaviors is a part of this. Here is one way to consider your own biases:

- Choose a specific social group identity that you are *not* a part of; it could be related to culture, language, gender, race, economic class, or religion. Make a list of all the biases or stereotypes you have ever heard about this group of people. Don't censor yourself. Write them down regardless of whether you believe them. (You cannot change your thinking or gain new knowledge unless you first uncover and face the messages that have surrounded you throughout your life.)

- Choose two or three items from your list and think about how, where, and from whom you learned these biased messages. Share your thinking with a colleague.

- How much real contact did you or do you have with people who are members of the identity group you are thinking about?

- How do your own social identities influence the implicit biases you learned?

Conclusion

Understanding who you are and how you came to be the person you now are gives you a deeper understanding of how children develop and what factors helped to shape them. This is a lifelong process. Teachers are on a continual journey of self-discovery as they work with children, families, and coworkers who sometimes reflect their own experiences and sometimes challenge them. Recognizing how your actions support or contradict the stereotypes that hurt children and families is an essential step in creating a program—and indeed, a world—in which every child is fully supported and flourishes.

About the Authors

Louise Derman-Sparks, MA, has worked with children and adults in early childhood education for more than 50 years and is a faculty emeritus of Pacific Oaks College. She is coauthor of several books, including *Leading Anti-Bias Early Childhood Programs: A Guide for Change, Anti-Bias Education for Young Children and Ourselves,* and *Teaching/Learning Anti-Racism: A Developmental Approach.*

Julie Olsen Edwards, coauthor of *Anti-Bias Education for Young Children and Ourselves,* was on the faculty of Cabrillo College's early childhood education department for 45 years. A lifetime activist for children and families, she continues to write, teach, and consult on issues of equity, diversity, and anti-bias.

Catherine M. Goins is assistant superintendent of early childhood education for Placer County Office of Education and a community college instructor.

naeyc®
Accreditation

This chapter supports the following NAEYC Early Learning Program Accreditation Standards and Topic Areas:

Standard 1: Relationships
1.A Building Positive Relationships Between Teachers and Families
1.E Addressing Challenging Behaviors

Standard 3: Teaching
3.B Creating Caring Communities for Learning

Standard 6: Staff Competencies, Preparation, and Support
6.D Ongoing Professional Development

Developing Empathy to Build Warm, Inclusive Classrooms

Charis L. Wahman and Elizabeth A. Steed, with Susan Friedman

Modeling and teaching empathy—concern for others' feelings—is an important part of being an effective, culturally competent teacher. But research shows that teachers tend to be less empathetic with children who are from different racial, ethnic, and cultural backgrounds than their own. Fortunately, research also indicates that by building self-awareness, teachers can change, creating classroom environments that are equally warm and inclusive for all children.

This chapter is adapted from Price & Steed 2016.

The following tips can help you consider your assumptions, expectations, and biases so that you can better develop your own empathy and the children's as well.

1. Think About It

When teachers have unfavorable perceptions about children who differ from them (in terms of culture, race, or ethnic identity), children's learning is negatively impacted. For example, teachers tend to judge Black boys' boisterous, full body play as more aggressive than similar play among White boys. This contributes to Black boys being much more likely to be suspended or expelled than other preschoolers.

2. Make a Difference

Commit to self-reflection to uncover your personal biases and assumptions, and help bridge understanding across cultural groups.

3. Ask Yourself Hard Questions

Reflect on questions like "What are my initial reactions to this child and her family?," "What do those reactions tell me about my personal beliefs and assumptions?," "What can I do to build children's and families' trust?," and "How can I connect with them in meaningful ways?"

4. Model Warm and Responsive Actions

Greet children with a smile and welcoming words. Anticipate and promptly address children's needs and worries.

5. Highlight Respect, Kindness, Compassion, and Responsibility

Carefully select the books, games, music, and other materials in your lessons and activities. Help children discover similarities with peers from different backgrounds.

6. Build a Classroom Library that Features Diversity

Make sure the books include characters who reflect the many different identities of the children in your classroom. It's important for all children—particularly those of color—to see themselves in stories.

Each and Every Child

7. Invite Guests to Share Their Cultures, Traditions, and Talents

Tap into children's and families' interests and cultural resources by creating time and space for them to share their special skills and knowledge in the classroom.

8. Acknowledge Your Progress

Consider the changes you're making, and honor your journey. You are becoming a more culturally competent teacher who is deeply empathetic toward all the children in your class.

About the Authors

Charis L. (Price) Wahman, PhD, is assistant professor of special education at Michigan State University. Born and raised in Detroit, Michigan, Charis attended public school in an urban environment. As a professional, she has worked with young children and their families in urban contexts for over 10 years. She has published articles and presented on social and emotional development of young children.

Elizabeth A. Steed, PhD, is associate professor in the early childhood education program at the University of Colorado Denver. She has published articles, presented at conferences, and served on state leadership teams focused on improving the social and emotional competence of young children.

Susan Friedman is senior director of publishing and professional learning at NAEYC.

Accreditation

This chapter supports the following NAEYC Early Learning Program Accreditation Standards and Topic Areas:

Standard 1: Relationships
1.D Creating a Predictable, Consistent, and Harmonious Classroom

Standard 3: Teaching
3.B Creating Caring Communities for Learning

CHAPTER 3

Valuing Diversity

Developing a Deeper Understanding of All Young Children's Behavior

Barbara Kaiser and Judy Sklar Rasminsky

Everything we think, say, and do is processed through our own cultural backgrounds. But because culture is absorbed and passed down from generation to generation rather than explicitly taught, many of us may be unaware of it.

Culture shapes not only our values and beliefs but also our gender roles, family structures, languages, dress, food, etiquette, approaches to disabilities, child-rearing practices, and even our expectations for children's behavior. In this way, culture creates diversity.

Cultural Diversity and Teachers

For teachers, it is essential to see and understand your own culture in order to see and understand how the cultures of children and their families influence children's behavior. Only then can you give every child a fair chance to succeed.

Think about your own upbringing. How did your family's expectations affect what you did? Were your parents, siblings, and other relatives close or distant? Were they strict, lenient, or somewhere in between? Were your school's expectations any different? All of this, and more, plays a part in how you view the behavior of the children you teach.

These ideas lie at the heart of NAEYC's position statement "Advancing Equity in Early Childhood Education" (NAEYC 2019). Its guiding principles include

- Recognizing that "self-awareness, humility, respect, and a willingness to learn are key to becoming a teacher who equitably and effectively supports all children and families" (13)
- Developing a strong understanding of culture and diversity
- Understanding that "families are the primary context for children's development and learning" (13)

One major takeaway from the position statement is that early childhood educators must support consistently warm and caring relationships between families and their children, respect families' languages and cultures, and incorporate those languages and cultures into the curriculum, their teaching practices, and the learning environment.

Cultural Diversity and Young Children

Children bring their own set of culturally based expectations, skills, talents, abilities, and values with them into the classroom. And they begin to develop their self-concept (at least in part) from how others see them. To form positive self-concepts, children must honor and respect their own families and cultures and have others honor and respect these key facets of their identities too. If the classroom doesn't reflect and validate their families and cultures, children may feel invisible, unimportant, incompetent, and ashamed of who they are.

Many people, including educators, have long believed it is better to act color blind and/or "culture blind"—that is, to not acknowledge color or culture. But research has shown that this artificial blindness keeps us from recognizing, acknowledging, and appreciating important differences. Worse, it may lead to unintentional bias toward or disrespect for those who are different from us.

We know now that acknowledgments of color and culture are essential for legitimizing differences. Color and culture make each one of us special and enable us to offer unique gifts and opportunities to groups we are part of. At the same time, color and culture help children learn about each other and the world. In short, color and culture enrich classrooms.

To appreciate what each child can contribute to the class, teachers need to learn about each family's cultural values. Helping children to see themselves in your pedagogy, curriculum, environment, and materials enables them (and their families) to feel welcomed and valued.

Take a look around your classroom.

- Does the artwork on the walls accurately reflect the children's lives, or are the walls covered with store-bought, stereotypical images?
  - ✓ Why not have the children create their own posters with their own artwork, things from home, and photos families can supply?
- Are labels (and other child-focused texts) repeated in each child's home language, or are they in English only?
  - ✓ Why not forge connections and support children's learning by asking family members to help children use their home languages throughout the room?

It's important to see cultural and linguistic differences as resources, not as deficits. As NAEYC's position statement on advancing equity puts it, "Children's learning is facilitated when teaching practices, curricula, and learning environments build on children's strengths and are developmentally, culturally, and linguistically appropriate for each child" (NAEYC 2019, 13).

The Difference Between Equitable and Equal

Equal is not the same as equitable. Every child in your group has different needs, skills, interests, and abilities. *Equal* would mean giving all children the same activities, materials, and books. *Equitable* means ensuring that you consider each child's strengths, context, and needs and provide all children with the opportunities that will support them in reaching their potential.

It's crucial to recognize the inequities that children and their families face—in school and out. The position statement reminds us that "dominant social biases are rooted in the social, political, and economic structures of the United States. Powerful messages—conveyed through the media, symbols, attitudes, and actions—continue to reflect and promote both explicit and implicit bias" (NAEYC 2019, 14). For example, research conducted by Yale University professor Walter Gilliam clearly shows that young African American boys are subject to higher rates of suspension and expulsion than their White European American peers.

How Cultural Diversity Shapes Behavior

Your culture and the children's cultures aren't the only cultures at work in your classroom. Every school and early childhood education program has a culture too. The cultures of most American schools are based on White European American values. As the makeup of the US population becomes more diverse, there is more cultural dissonance—which impacts children's behavior.

White European American culture has an individual orientation that teaches children to function independently, stand out, talk about themselves, and view property as personal. In contrast, many other cultures value interdependence, fitting in, helping others and being helped, being modest, and sharing property. In fact, some languages have no words for *I*, *me*, or *mine*.

Children who find themselves in an unfamiliar environment—such as a classroom that reflects a culture different from their home culture—are likely to feel confused, isolated, alienated, conflicted, and less competent because what they've learned so far in their home culture simply doesn't apply. They may not understand the rules, or they may be unable to communicate their needs in the school's language.

Rethinking Challenging Behavior

Because your responses to children's conflicts and challenging behavior are culture bound, it is all too easy to misinterpret children's words or actions. The next time a child seems defiant, ask yourself, "Is that behavior culturally influenced? Could I be misunderstanding the child's words or actions?"

For example, White European Americans tend to use implicit commands, such as, "Johnny, can you please put the blocks away?" Children raised in the White European American culture understand that they are being told to put away the blocks. But children raised in the African American culture may interpret this utterance differently. In their culture, adult commands are usually explicit: "DuShane, put away the blocks." To African American children, an implicit command in the form of a question may seem to offer a choice about how to behave.

Culture also defines personal space, including how much space feels appropriate in the block area, at circle/meeting time, and in the dramatic play area. In some cultures, children feel comfortable playing close to one another; in others, the same space may feel claustrophobic and lead children to hit or shove a playmate who seems too near. Similarly, you may stand too close or too far away, depending on children's cultures. For example, if Cadence doesn't pay attention to your request to keep the sand in the sandbox, you may be too far away to connect with her.

In White European American culture, teachers expect children to sit still and maintain eye contact to show that they're paying attention. But in other cultures, children might show their interest by joining in; they may learn through hearing or telling a story, watching others, or using trial and error. If they don't understand the lesson, they might have a hard time paying attention. Or they may be paying attention in a different way.

Culture Counts

There are many rewards for teachers who take culture into account. You can form authentic, caring relationships with children and families; build connections between what children already know and what they need to know; select activities, materials, and instructional strategies that honor children's cultures and life experiences; and teach children the skills they need to succeed in a global society.

About the Authors

Barbara Kaiser and **Judy Sklar Rasminsky** are the authors of *Challenging Behavior in Young Children: Understanding, Preventing, and Responding Effectively,* now in its fourth edition (Pearson Education, 2017). Learn more about their work at their website (www.challengingbehavior.com) and their blog (https://childrenwithchallengingbehavior.com).

Photographs: pp. 18, 20, 22, © Getty Images

Accreditation

This chapter supports the following NAEYC Early Learning Program Accreditation Standards and Topic Areas:

Standard 1: Relationships
1.A Building Positive Relationships Between Teachers and Families

Standard 7: Families
7.A Knowing and Understanding the Program's Families

Recognize and be prepared to provide different levels of support to different children depending on what they need. For example, some children may need more attention at certain times or more support for learning particular concepts or skills. Differentiating support in a strengths-based way is the most equitable approach because it helps to meet each child's needs.

Consider the developmental, cultural, and linguistic appropriateness of the learning environment and your teaching practices for each child. Offer meaningful, relevant, and appropriately challenging activities across all interests and abilities. Children of all genders, with and without disabilities, should see themselves and their families, languages, and cultures regularly and meaningfully reflected in the environment and learning materials. Counter common stereotypes and misinformation. Remember that the learning environment and its materials reflect what you do and do not value by what is present and what is omitted.

PART 2

Creating an Equitable Classroom

How do you support the learning of all the children you teach? Do you consider the languages children speak? Their cultures and family structures? Do some children need particular support related to their language development, while others need extra time and attention when it comes to learning math or science? Have the children in your class generally had similar experiences to support their learning, such as museum visits, weekends playing outdoors, and bedtime reading routines? Or do their experiences vary widely, meaning the children need different levels of scaffolding and a variety of strategies to bolster their learning in specific areas?

Equity is not a one-size-fits-all approach, and teaching with an equity lens is a complex undertaking. It means making intentional decisions about how you set up your classroom environment, what books you include in the reading center, what you put on your walls, and who you invite into your classroom. It means engaging in careful observation and documentation of children's play and learning, and knowing when to provide support, when to scaffold children's learning with specific materials and experiences, and when to step back so children can explore on their own.

The chapters in this section share ideas from a range of educators about how they approach teaching with an equity lens. Some content emphasizes the need to adapt materials and approaches to support children who speak different languages or who have recently come from other countries as refugees. Other chapters outline specific strategies, such as guided play, to support children's language and knowledge development. Many of the ideas explored here can be implemented in or adapted for your own classrooms.

Read and Reflect

As you read the chapters in this section, consider and evaluate your own classroom practices using these reflection questions.

1. Chapters 4 (page 29) and 5 (page 33) describe the importance of carefully selecting and incorporating materials in the classroom as part of guided play. Look at the centers in your own classroom and think about what sort of play materials might encourage children, particularly emergent bilingual learners, to use new vocabulary words from books you are reading or themes you are studying. After including some of these materials, observe how the children use them and then reflect on your observations. Did you hear children using new vocabulary? How did you balance engaging with the children to encourage their use of new vocabulary and stepping back so they could continue their play?

2. As Chapter 6 (page 39) highlights, establishing trust and maintaining strong bonds with refugee children are key to making them feel included and nurtured in your classroom. Reflect on some ways you have done this or brainstorm some ways you could foster supportive relationships with refugee children you teach and their families. If you do not currently serve any refugee children, are there other children in your classroom who might benefit from these approaches?

3. One of the tips for creating a culturally responsive STEAM curriculum covered in Chapter 7 (page 45) recommends including books and images that feature scientists, mathematicians, and engineers of various races, ethnicities, cultures, and genders. Why do you think this is important? As you look around your own classroom and walk the halls of your school, what do you notice about the roles and ethnicities depicted? Is there anything you think should be changed?

4. After reading Chapter 8 (page 49), evaluate the various areas in your classroom and choose one (a center, the outdoor play area, a bookshelf) to consider more specifically. With DECAL (**D**ifferent **E**xperiences, **C**ultures, **A**bilities, and **L**anguages) in mind, what about this area might you adjust and how?

5. Try a few of the ideas for helping children develop storytelling skills outlined in Chapter 9 (page 55). What were the results? Why do you think providing children with opportunities to tell stories connects to equity?

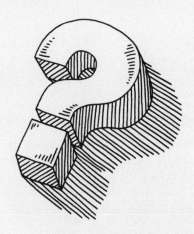

CHAPTER 4

Connecting Culture and Play

Practical Strategies for Educators

Kamini Kamdar

"Wait, we don't throw rice over our heads!" I explained to Kavya, a junior kindergarten student (4 years old) who was playing at the sensory bin. I had filled the bin with rice and buried alphabet letters for the children to discover. I had imagined the children quietly exploring, finding hidden letters, and becoming curious about them—perhaps even identifying some letters.

But the children had imagined something quite different! Just as I was about to suggest some new ideas for playing with the rice, another child joined in with Kavya. They giggled, gleefully tossing rice. I wondered if our sensory bin was such a good idea.

Shortly after redirecting both children to another activity, I realized Kavya was not throwing rice—she was mimicking a custom commonly practiced in South Asian cultures. I thought back to the many South Asian cultural ceremonies I had attended as a child and remembered seeing rice thrown over the heads of newly married couples and newborn babies. Then I had an aha moment: Kavya was playing with the rice in a way that was meaningful to her.

"Is this what you do with rice sometimes at home?" I asked. Kavya nodded and smiled. We both laughed and began to dig for letters together in the sensory bin. While I was glad that I had recognized what Kavya was doing, I knew I needed to do more to embrace all of the children's cultures.

Both English and the child's home language (German) are included in the title of his clay sculpture.

Ein Fuchs (A fox) by Marvin

Bringing Home Cultures into the Classroom

Reflecting on my interactions with Kavya, I realized that it was a special moment for me. It reminded me to carefully consider the diverse cultures in our learning community when planning classroom activities. I decided to actively incorporate a variety of strategies into my teaching practice to connect cultures and playful learning.

I wanted to go beyond stocking our classroom library with stories about celebrations such as Lunar New Year, Diwali, and Kwanzaa. Stories are a great starting point, but I wanted to go deeper by creating a classroom that embraces the diversity of our community through different languages, foods, textiles, decorations, and traditions.

Over time, I asked families to contribute photographs and descriptions of their cultural celebrations. I encouraged the children to write in their home languages (as well as in English) in their journals and to share their languages by teaching their classmates frequently used words, such as those for feelings, numbers, and classroom materials.

Our sense of community grew and was enriched even more than I had hoped. It was wonderful to see our classroom shift from one that was cocreated with the children to one that was cocreated with the children and their families.

I now see how important it is to recognize the knowledge, values, and ideas young children bring with them from home and from their cultural communities. It's also crucial to create spaces in the classroom where all of the children's cultural practices are represented, validated, and appreciated.

Incorporating Cultures into Play

Sharing diverse cultures through play has become a strong focus of my teaching. I actively seek out new and meaningful ways for the children in our classroom to feel proud of their cultural backgrounds and to continue learning about them. As the world around us becomes increasingly diverse, it's so important for young children to see themselves meaningfully reflected in classrooms—and to have positive experiences learning about their own and their classmates' cultures.

Our reading corner includes a variety of fabrics with prints that reflect the different cultures of the children in our classroom.

Here are some ideas to connect cultures and play in a learning environment:

- Create a collaborative art installation—for example, a quilt that showcases the diverse backgrounds of learners in the classroom or school by asking families to contribute culturally meaningful fabrics.

- Look for interesting artifacts to place around the classroom to spark conversation. Consider different types of kitchen tools, dual language books, books originally published in other countries, and learning materials—including toys!—from other countries.

- Be sensitive to the meanings behind some commonly used items; rice, lentils, and natural materials all have special significance in many South Asian and First Nations cultures. While getting to know all people's traditions and values may not be possible, educators can learn what is important to the children and families in their programs.

- Invite families and community elders into the classroom to share stories or fables from their cultures. It's amazing how many different tales each culture has, and it's really neat for children to hear them! And by documenting the stories and talking with children about them over time, the class will see similarities in themes and values across cultures. Some teachers and children may even retell and illustrate the stories to create their own storybooks, developing a rich and unique classroom library.

- Encourage families and children to share photographs of cultural celebrations. We display family photographs in our classroom and use them as opportunities for meaningful writing and conversation. As the school year progresses, our collection grows—it's wonderful to observe!

To create our collaborative quilt, we asked families to contribute fabrics they felt reflected their cultural backgrounds. The quilt now hangs in our school foyer, which is a great way to welcome children and their families into the school's diverse community.

Conclusion

Exploring cultures through playful learning helps create authentic, positive learning experiences for young children, valuing the knowledge and traditions children and families bring to the classroom. It also ensures that teaching practices in early childhood education institutions are democratic. When teachers include the voices of young children and their families, they create a space for children to shape their own identities as learners.

About the Author

Kamini Kamdar is a PhD student at York University and a kindergarten teacher in Toronto, Ontario. She is interested in global philosophies of early childhood education and connecting research with practical strategies to support early childhood educators. She regularly blogs at www.teachgrowlove.com.

Photographs: p. 28, © Getty Images; pp. 30, 31, 32, courtesy of the author

naeyc®
Accreditation

This chapter supports the following NAEYC Early Learning Program Accreditation Standards and Topic Areas:

Standard 3: Teaching
3.A Designing Enriched Learning Environments

Standard 7: Families
7.A Knowing and Understanding the Program's Families

CHAPTER 5

The Balancing Act of Guided Play

Brenna Hassinger-Das, Kathy Hirsh-Pasek, and Roberta Michnick Golinkoff

Editors' Note

Preschool teachers value children's play, but they also want to effectively bolster children's language and math skills so children can reach their full potential. Guided play experiences combine child-directed play and exploration with light scaffolding from the teacher to maximize children's learning. Guided play is not an adult taking over a child's play or direct instruction, but it also is not simply child-directed play where the teacher doesn't engage at all. What makes guided play so effective is that it offers a way for an adult to provide immediate and direct feedback during a time in which a child is fully interested and motivated.

During guided play, teachers engage with children in limited but specific ways before stepping back and observing children as they continue with their self-directed play. It takes careful planning to set up the learning environment and observe the children. This chapter, adapted from the authors' article "The Case of Brain Science and Play: A Developing Story" (published in the May 2017 issue of *Young Children*), highlights just how powerful play is in helping children be mentally active, engaged, and socially interactive as well as building meaningful connections to their lives.

—Susan Friedman and Alissa Mwenelupembe

This chapter is adapted from Hassinger-Das, Hirsh-Pasek, & Golinkoff 2017.

Ms. Elena's Head Start classroom is filled with eager 3- and 4-year-olds. It's center time, and the children have split into small groups. At one center, Ms. Elena has carefully selected play materials—including a barn, a chicken coop, and animal figurines—that reflect the story lines and specific vocabulary words from books she read aloud related to farm life as part of the class's storybook theme of the week. While Ms. Elena looks on, Sara, Javon, and Ashish arrive at the center and immediately pick up the toys. They each choose a figurine and begin playing. Sara says to Javon, "I'll be the cow!" Javon says, "Okay, then I'll be the chicken. I'm going to go sleep in the coop. The cow should go sleep in the barn." Ashish says, "Then I'll be the horse, and I'll go sleep in the barn too."

Together, the three children move their figurines to the coop and the barn while making mooing, clucking, and neighing sounds. Since *coop* was one of the week's focus words, Ms. Elena joins in the children's play, making sure that Sara and Ashish understand the word as well as Javon: "Sleeping in the coop sounds like a great idea, Javon! A *coop* is a house for chickens. Remember when we saw a coop on our field trip to Maple Farm? Javon, Sara, and Ashish, where do you think the chickens would live if we didn't have a coop on the farm?" Ashish says, "I think they live in the barn!" Then Sara says, "Yes, they live in the barn, because it's nice and warm inside there." Ms. Elena says, "That sounds like a really good place for the chickens to live if we didn't have a coop!"

At this point, Ms. Elena steps back and the children take up a new direction for the play. She continues to listen for ways to build on the children's interests and reinforce their weekly focus words during the session without interrupting their play.

Why Play?

Free play and guided play—together known as *playful learning*—are tools through which children can learn in joyful and rich ways. A growing body of behavioral research establishes relationships between children's play and development in several areas, including language, mathematics and spatial skills, scientific thinking, and social and emotional development.

Play includes the four key ingredients of successful learning: learning occurs best when children are *mentally active* (not passive), *engaged* (not distracted), *socially interactive* (with peers or adults), and building *meaningful connections* to their lives.

These features are evident in Ms. Elena's classroom in the opening vignette. Javon was mentally active when he thought about where he learned the name of the place where chickens sleep and then uses the word *coop* appropriately. Sara was engaged when she chose to be the cow and moved in concert with Javon and Ashish instead of being distracted by other groups at play. Ms. Elena made the word *coop* more meaningful for the children by making a connection to when the children visited Maple Farm. Finally, the children were socially interactive when they built a play scenario that involved all three of them, with Ms. Elena joining in as a scaffolder.

These kinds of playful interactions between children and adults may be essential for creating the supportive environments necessary for healthy social and emotional development. Guided play in particular features this type of social interaction and has demonstrated promising outcomes for learning and development.

What is Guided Play?

Today, most researchers agree that play is fun, flexible, voluntary, and self motivated; it involves active engagement and often incorporates make-believe. Guided play maintains the joyful child-directed aspects of free play but adds an additional focus on learning goals through light adult scaffolding. It offers an opportunity for exploration in a context specifically designed to foster a learning goal. As such, it features two important elements: child agency (the child directs the learning) and gentle adult guidance to ensure that the child progresses toward the learning goal. Research suggests that guided play is a successful teaching tool. Here are some ways guided play can work in the classroom to build specific language, mathematics, and spatial skills.

Language Development

The play scenario in the opening vignette describing Ms. Elena's class offers an excellent example of a teacher intentionally scaffolding children's vocabulary development through guided play. This is an especially effective way to bolster preschoolers' vocabulary development, especially for young children from disadvantaged backgrounds.

One study tested the effectiveness of vocabulary learning through guided play when compared to a more teacher-directed learning activity. Children participated in shared book reading and then reviewed half of the vocabulary words through guided play and the other half through a teacher-directed picture card word-recall activity. The guided play resembled the learning taking place in the opening vignette. After play-based word learning, children defined the target words more readily than they did after picture card-based word learning.

Tips for Getting Started with Guided Play

- Add play materials to your classroom that will encourage children's use of specific vocabulary. For example, Ms. Elena added farm animal toys.

- Think of your interactions with children as feedback. Observe and wait for an opportunity to introduce and use a new vocabulary word as they play. Then step back and observe if they incorporate the new word.

- Wait for the right movement to offer feedback. For example, as a child stacks blocks that continually fall down, call attention to the size of the blocks. Ask which ones are larger and which are smaller and if the smaller or larger ones are falling. Then step back and observe the child continuing to experiment after your light guidance.

Mathematics and Spatial Skills

Guided play is also effective for fostering spatial skills—important in and of themselves and also tied to later mathematics success. For example, a study with preschoolers compared children's ability to learn about geometry and shapes through guided play, free play, and direct instruction. In the guided play scenario, the adult followed the children's lead and scaffolded the interaction. Children learned more about geometry and shapes than those participating in either the direct instruction condition (where the children listened passively while the adult delivered the content in a fun way) or the free play condition (where children interacted with the shapes in whatever way they wished).

To envision how a similar effect might occur in the classroom, imagine a different center in Ms. Elena's room:

> Pablo, Keisha, and Nari arrive at a table filled with tiles of different shapes. They all pick up pieces and begin snapping Magna-Tiles together. Nari says, "I'm going to build a tower! I can't get these pieces to fit." Ms. Elena is observing the children and chooses this moment to join in and say, "What shapes do you have, Nari?" Pablo says, "Nari has a square." "That's right, Pablo. Nari has a square. Nari, can you find another square?" Nari holds up a square. Ms. Elena says, "What makes that a square?" She pauses to let the children think about it, then continues, "It has four sides that are all the same length." She then says, "I wonder if it's possible to make a bigger square using the pieces you are holding up." Keisha says, "Hmm . . . I want to try!" The children look at each other and lay the pieces down—eventually discovering that by putting all four of the squares together, they create a larger square. Ms. Elena notices their discovery, and says, "Wow! You made a bigger square! It still has four sides, and all of the sides are the same length."

Ms. Elena wove the definition of a square into the children's play without taking over, but she also encouraged the children to push themselves to make an important discovery about the shape tiles. Guided play allows teachers to piggyback on children's joy and engagement to reinforce important skills.

Why Does Guided Play Work?

Guided play increases children's knowledge through opportunities to receive immediate, meaningful adult feedback. It is also an ideal example of active, engaged, meaningful, and socially interactive learning. Consider, for instance, children playing with a shape sorter. The children discuss how to insert the shapes so that the sorter lights up. They keep inserting shapes and notice that sometimes the sorter lights up and sometimes it doesn't, but they can't figure out why. Their teacher joins in and makes some gentle guiding suggestions to help them by asking what the children have already tried and what they could try next. As children incorporate this feedback while continuing to experiment, they generate hypotheses and draw causal connections, becoming little scientists. Play helps children discover causal relationships through experimentation. Intentional, light guidance and scaffolding from thoughtful adults, when needed, prevents frustration and enables the children to engage in longer periods of playful experimentation.

The Science Behind Guided Play

Adult-scaffolded play experiences might be particularly important because they actually help children develop a part of their brain that uses clues from the environment to help the brain figure out what might happen next. Guided play might foster a psychological *mise en place*—a term derived from the culinary world meaning "everything in its place"—which helps children prepare their minds to embrace learning experiences in a positive way. Ms. Elena cultivated such a *mise en place* through her inclusion of farm-focused play activities. By preparing the play environment to support her teaching goal (the children learning the farm related focus words), Ms. Elena allowed children to work toward this goal in their own playful way. This type of gently scaffolded, playful learning fosters children's desire to seek out similar meaningful learning opportunities.

Conclusion

Everyone plays, and growing research shows that play likely has a significant role in young children's development and their understanding of how the world works. As we await new discoveries from brain science, one finding is already clear: Play is a wonderful context for active, engaged, meaningful, and socially interactive learning.

About the Authors

Brenna Hassinger-Das, PhD, is assistant professor of psychology at Pace University, in New York City. Her research examines children's play and learning in home, school, and community contexts, particularly for children experiencing poverty.

Kathy Hirsh-Pasek, PhD, is the Stanley and Debra Lefkowitz Faculty Fellow in the Department of Psychology at Temple University and is a senior fellow at the Brookings Institution. She is committed to bridging the gap between research and application.

Roberta Michnick Golinkoff, PhD, is the Unidel H. Rodney Sharp Professor of Education, Psychology, and Linguistics at the University of Delaware, in Newark. She has written numerous articles and books and lectures internationally about language development, playful learning, and spatial development.

Accreditation

This chapter supports the following NAEYC Early Learning Program Accreditation Standards and Topic Areas:

Standard 1: Relationships
1.C Helping Children Make Friends

Standard 2: Curriculum
2.B Social and Emotional Development

Standard 3: Teaching
3.A Designing Enriched Learning Environments
3.E Responding to Children's Interests and Needs
3.G Using Instruction to Deepen Children's Understanding and Build Their Skills and Knowledge

CHAPTER 6

Welcoming Refugee Children into Early Childhood Classrooms

Sadia Warsi

In Mr. Allen's pre-K class, the children greet their classmates in each other's home language. Seth turns to Maryam and greets her in Arabic, "*Assalamu Aliakum.*" Maryam very softly says back, "Hello," in English. Tarek says, "*Buenos días,*" and Isabella responds, "*Günaydın,*" in Turkish.

Refugee families are a part of many communities, and they bring rich cultural experiences to early learning programs. Because of the social and emotional impact that being a refugee has on young children and their families, it is important that early childhood educators create inclusive and nurturing classroom environments.

Most children who are refugees have experienced hardship and trauma, so it's vital that they feel welcomed by teachers and peers in their new classrooms. Here are some ideas to get you started.

Prepare to Greet the Children

Work with the class to be ready to greet their new classmate in a warm and cheerful manner and to show appreciation for the child's culture. The children can learn the new child's name and how to say a few words in his or her language. They can create welcome cards and pictures for their new classmate.

Create Play Experiences that Do Not Require English

All children need opportunities to play in the classroom. If new arrivals do not speak English, it will take them some time to learn the language. In the meantime, ensure that there are games and activities available that don't require much language. Offer board games and art experiences that need little instruction (simple games, such as Candyland, and open-ended art materials). Plan activities in which children engage in creative and imaginative play using music and movement.

Here are some play-based activities for dual language learners:

- Photograph all the children in the classroom. Make a copy of each photo, and play a matching game. Write the children's names at the bottom of their photos to help them recognize their own and each other's names.
- Children can create their own musical instruments and form bands. Make maracas by filling plastic bottles with beans, create string instruments by wrapping large rubber bands around open shoe boxes, and use a comb and tissue paper to make a kazoo. Children can compose music together and invite their families to a gig.

Play-based activities help create an environment where children can work together without the need for frequent teacher mediation. This environment offers opportunities for children to connect and helps new classmates adjust to the classroom.

Familiarize Families with Classrooms

Many families—whether refugees or immigrants—come from countries where school experiences are very different from those in the United States. All families want to be involved and support their children in their new school. But sometimes it's hard for families with little or no prior school experience within early childhood settings to understand how to begin. And it can be especially confusing for families from different cultural backgrounds, who speak another language. Consider using visuals to introduce culturally and linguistically diverse families to the school environment. (See "A Picture's Worth a Thousand Words" on page 41.)

If an interpreter is available or you can communicate verbally, talk with the parents and other caregivers about what to expect. Explain classroom routines, such as arrival and departure and the daily schedule. Talk about classroom rules. Many children who are refugees have spent unstructured time in camps or other transitional settings. Help them become part of the structured classroom routine as soon as possible.

Once they spend time in the classroom and observe their children's daily activities, families will feel more at ease and will be able to reinforce those routines at home. Inviting families and caregivers into the classroom helps build home–school relationships and encourages them to be active partners in their children's education.

Connect with Related Community Cultural Groups

Many children and teachers may not have interacted with diverse cultural groups from other countries—and particularly from countries suffering through war, famine, and other crises. It's difficult to understand the experiences of children who are refugees without first understanding their home cultures. And it also helps to be aware that there are different cultural groups within every country. One resource may be individuals who work closely with refugee families in the United States. They can offer information about particular cultures and help teachers better understand the experiences of children who are refugees.

Families who have escaped horrific conditions are not always comfortable talking about political situations in their home countries. Refugee families are trying to create a new sense of peace and calm in the lives of their children. They want to preserve their children's childhood and create new memories and positive beginnings.

Meeting Emotional Needs

Many families and preschools try to shield children from harmful images and experiences so as not to overburden them emotionally. However, children who have lived in war zones and other fraught settings have experienced trauma beyond their years and may become overwhelmed and emotionally vulnerable in certain situations.

With preschoolers, typical conflicts arise while sharing materials or taking turns. They may use inappropriate language when trying to resolve these conflicts. It should come as no surprise that children who have experienced trauma may have an extra-difficult time working through common classroom conflicts. It's important to guide them in successful problem solving so they learn that they will not be punished when they make a mistake or have an outburst. It also helps all children if there is a quiet space to go to calm down, like the classroom library beanbag chair.

Establish One-on-One Time with Children Who Are Refugees

It's not uncommon for young children to feel lost in the classroom and to miss their families. This can be exceptionally hard for children who are refugees, because they tend to have strong attachments to their families and may have shared traumatic experiences together. One of the biggest fears many children have is losing their parents—and some may actually have lost a parent or a loved one. A few times a day, reassure children that they are safe and that their parents or caregivers will return at the end of the day. Establishing trust and maintaining a strong bond with them is key to settling refugee children in your classroom. Build with blocks or draw together during centers time. You don't need to talk much if language is a barrier.

Create Opportunities for Refugee Families to Share Their Traditions

As refugee families adjust to school and their children become comfortable with their peers, you might invite the parents or caregivers to share some of their traditions, such as celebrations, music, food, native clothing, and folktales. Offer activities like creating ornaments or other arts and crafts from their home countries. Support families by gathering materials in advance, making sure that participating doesn't cause a financial burden. Celebrate all the different cultures represented in the classroom so refugee families don't feel singled out.

Conclusion

You will find that refugee families are grateful and appreciate your support. They are eager to cooperate and collaborate to ensure that their children fit into the classroom and maintain their connections to their rich cultures.

About the Author

Sadia Warsi, PhD, is associate professor of early childhood and special education at National Louis University in Chicago.

naeyc®
Accreditation
™

This chapter supports the following NAEYC Early Learning Program Accreditation Standards and Topic Areas:

Standard 1: Relationships
1.A Building Positive Relationships Between Teachers and Families

Standard 3: Teaching
3.F Making Learning Meaningful for All Children

Standard 7: Families
7.A Knowing and Understanding the Program's Families

Standard 8: Community Relationships
8.A Linking with the Community

CHAPTER 7

Creating a Culturally Responsive STEAM Curriculum

Anthony Broughton and Michiko B. McClary

As a preschool teacher, you know it's important to affirm all children by bringing their cultures into the classroom. You also know that, starting in early childhood, all children need to develop knowledge and skills in the STEAM subjects—science, technology, engineering, arts, and mathematics. Lots of preschool teachers think of being culturally responsive and teaching STEAM as separate goals, but they don't have to be! The following tips can support you in creating a culturally responsive STEAM curriculum.

1. Invite a Diverse Mix of Community Helpers to Visit Your Classroom

Invite engineers, architects, masons, construction workers, or others in careers related to the sciences and arts from various racial, ethnic, and cultural backgrounds to visit your classroom and enhance your STEAM curriculum. The children's family members and businesses in the local community are likely to have plenty of options. These community helpers can share their knowledge to support children in exploring STEAM topics (simple machines, electrical wiring, house building) in ways that are culturally meaningful. They may also bring in tools they use every day to perform their jobs, and they can share their STEAM experiences in ways that spark children's curiosity.

2. Honor Cultural Knowledge

Family and community members from various cultural backgrounds have a wealth of knowledge and experiences they can share to support the curriculum. Invite children's family members and people from the community who are gardeners, farmers, park rangers, or botanists to share how they use STEAM concepts every day to cultivate healthy plants and habitats. Inform these classroom visitors of the concepts you are teaching so they can help children make meaningful connections. For example, they may help you integrate your unit about plants across the curriculum in culturally relevant ways, which is important because plants have different meanings and are used for various purposes (medicine, rituals) across cultures.

Each and Every Child

3. Connect with Technology

Use technology to show STEAM in different settings across the world. Some websites explore engineering concepts used by various cultures, such as showing how the Egyptians built pyramids and how nomadic Native American tribes build teepees. Or, hold video conferences on a computer or mobile device with STEAM community helpers to have them share their knowledge with children remotely. For example, after a construction worker visits the classroom, the children could take a virtual field trip to the construction site by video conferencing. (For more examples of websites that explore engineering concepts, from an introduction to different types of buildings to in-depth explorations of pyramid and bridge construction, see https://bit.ly/2ml3CBF, https://to.pbs.org/2mjeb8i, and https://bit.ly/2md2dwL.

4. Empower Children with Culturally Responsive STEAM Images

Provide picture books and other images that feature scientists, mathematicians, and engineers of various races, ethnicities, cultures, and genders to empower all children. To further their anti-bias education, children should see and learn about STEAM professionals in nontraditional roles, such as Mae Jemison, an African American female astronaut.

5. Express STEAM Through Cultural Art

Invite local architects or artists from children's families to illustrate STEAM concepts through art. They could bring models of structures used to solve engineering problems or share ways they use art (drawings, photography, videography) to convey STEAM concepts. While this type of multimodal engagement is especially helpful for some children with learning disabilities, all children can benefit from multiple representations of concepts (video clips, pictures, models, speakers, books). You can extend art in the classroom by supporting children in creating blueprints of the structures they intend to build during block play.

You can also display drawings, paintings, or photographs of cultural structures (such as the Great Pyramid of Giza, the Great Wall of China, the Islamic Kaaba, the Roman Colosseum, the National Museum of African American History and Culture, and relevant structures from the local community) in the classroom. When children ask questions about these images, you can help them explore the structures through multiple perspectives, like architecture, engineering, history, and culture.

6. Connect Math at Home to the Classroom

Discover how children's families use mathematics in their homes. For example, from hair braids to jewelry to fabrics (like kente cloths), African American families have a rich variety of geometric patterns to share with the class. Families may also share recipes for traditional cultural dishes or beverages in which they use mathematical concepts like time, measurement, and counting. As families share ways they use math in their homes, create a class family math book to add to the class library.

7. Incorporate Cultural Books

Include culturally relevant books in the classroom that highlight STEAM concepts. Books like *Changing Seasons*, by Mon Trice; *Ada Twist, Scientist*, by Andrea Beaty; *Gathering the Sun: An Alphabet Book in Spanish and English,* by Alma Flor Ada; and *I Live in Tokyo*, by Mari Takabayashi, can be used to highlight different STEAM concepts. For example, *I Live in Tokyo* features different cultural buildings and structures unique to Tokyo. After reading it with the class, you could add the book as well as materials for drawing blueprints to the block center and encourage children to pretend to be architects and construction workers, building their own Tokyo-inspired structures.

8. Launch a Family STEAM Invention Project

Encourage families to create an invention that will make a positive impact on their community and the world. Have children brainstorm creative inventions. Using art, families can draw, paint, or create models of their STEAM invention to share with the class. Families can also gather ideas from picture books. For example, the books *Rainbow Weaver/Tejedora del arcoíris*, by Linda Elovitz Marshall, and *What Do They Do with All That Poo?* by Jane Kurtz, can give families insight into how different things are reused. The book *Ada Twist, Scientist*, by Andrea Beaty, has plenty of ideas for easy science projects to do at home.

9. Continue to Learn About Children's Cultures

Each child in your classroom is different. The best way to be culturally responsive is to get to know the children and learn about the cultural knowledge, perspectives, and values they each possess. Visit their communities and observe opportunities for teachable moments to enhance and extend your STEAM curriculum.

About the Authors

Anthony Broughton, PhD, is assistant professor of education and early childhood coordinator at Claflin University in Orangeburg, South Carolina.

Michiko B. McClary, PhD, is assistant professor of science education at Claflin University.

naeyc®
Accreditation

This chapter supports the following NAEYC Early Learning Program Accreditation Standard and Topic Areas:

Standard 2: Curriculum
2.G Science
2.H Technology

CHAPTER 8

Including All Children in Making and Tinkering!

Karen N. Nemeth and Pamela Brillante

Imagine a young child whose first language isn't English, who comes from a different cultural background, or who has a developmental delay or disability. She is away from home in a class where she can't communicate with other children or with the teachers. Things are happening all around her that are confusing and unfamiliar, and she is unable to participate fully with the other children. With the open-ended experiences of making and tinkering, you can give a child like this access to a whole world of learning and expression.

Bridging Languages

Like all children their age, preschoolers who are dual language learners (DLLs) have a wealth of knowledge and experience. But because their learning has been in their home language, they may not be able to express their knowledge in English. Making and tinkering gives children a chance to reveal their ingenuity and skill, amazing their teachers and classmates—and sometimes themselves. With open-ended materials and activities, DLLs can dive in and explore how objects work, how they go together, how they can be sorted, and how they can be used to express almost anything. Words are unnecessary—but can definitely be added!

Because language differences may affect how children work together, be ready to scaffold interactions between children. Sometimes DLLs need time to work quietly, without feeling pressured to talk. At other times, you can use making and tinkering to build language and concept learning, based on a child's individual interests. Provide words and questions in home languages that the child can later connect to new words in English. What's important about these experiences is that they give DLLs a way to feel successful and included—there are no limits to what they can do and no judgment about whether they are doing it right.

Each and Every Child

Sharing Cultures

Makerspaces offer a unique way to make a classroom culturally responsive. Invite families to visit your makerspace or to view videos or photos of it—they may come up with ideas they can contribute. Or send home a materials wish list (clean cardboard is always welcome). Request cereal boxes, packaging, magazines, and newspapers with words and images from other countries and in children's home languages. Ask families to send in kitchen utensils (disposable chopsticks are great for making and tinkering) or supplies they use in their hobbies or their work. Remember, a child's culture is really about the people and things that are part of his everyday life, home, and community. If a family loves to go fishing, then fishing supplies are part of that child's culture. Maybe the family can offer fishing line, weights, or flies to use in the makerspace. Making and tinkering is much more fun when there are both objects children recognize and things that are new to them.

Including All Abilities

Since making and tinkering materials and activities can be used in many ways, they offer opportunities for children of all abilities to play together. Many adaptations that make an experience accessible for children with disabilities can enhance other children's experiences as well. For example, a communication board—a chart with symbols or pictures of frequently used words or processes (*sit down, hungry, bathroom*)—supports communication for children with limited expressive language ability. Children communicate using the board by pointing and gesturing or staring at the symbols and pictures. This tool can also be useful for DLLs—or anyone! Teachers can create a making and tinkering board and include symbols for glue, scissors, string, and tape.

Some children need more advanced experiences that challenge their strength and dexterity. Others may need materials that require less strength or fine motor control. Large nuts and bolts, small nuts and bolts, and items made of heavy metal and light plastic can all be included and tried by all children. Be sure to think ahead: Take a mental survey of the class, then include materials, set up spaces, and provide additional support and adaptations that accommodate everyone.

Tips for Supporting Every Maker

To create a makerspace that works for every child in your classroom, strive for DECAL, or opportunities for children with Different Experiences, Cultures, Abilities, and Languages. These children may have different ways of understanding, holding, and using making and tinkering materials, so additional supports and adaptations may be needed to fully include everyone in the experience.

Nurture Social and Emotional Development

✓ Allow plenty of time for children to get into tinkering and figure out what they want to do.

✓ Set up teams of children who can help each other and work well together. When possible, pair children who speak the same language.

✓ Encourage children who have different skill levels with tools and materials to work together and help each other.

✓ Provide alternative activities (picture books); some children will need to take a break.

✓ Avoid using food, such as dried pasta and rice, in makerspaces. This is confusing for children who may not have enough to eat at home.

Consider Motor Needs

✓ Add some materials that require strong muscles, like real clay, and some that are easy to manipulate, like homemade playdough.

✓ Make tinkering surfaces accessible for wheelchairs, walkers, and standing frames.

✓ Include small items that require fine motor work (small beads and string) as well as larger items that can be explored by children with less coordination (large beads and stiff wire).

✓ Plan proactively for accessible materials and experiences that will include each child.

Support Language Skills

✓ Make a video showing examples of free exploration with found materials—not every child has experience with open-ended exploring and tinkering.

✓ Use photos and video to capture the learning process. How are children trying new things and making discoveries?

✓ Post words in English and home languages for adults to use as they talk with children about their materials and work.

✓ Model tinkering for children who speak different languages and those who have diverse abilities. Show that it's about trying out their ideas and making new discoveries.

✓ Support conversations as children learn to communicate with each other about their projects.

✓ Ask simple questions in children's home languages, and record their answers for translation later.

✓ Extend learning and support vocabulary practice throughout the day by choosing books and materials related to what's happening in the makerspace.

✓ Create a picture communication board so children can show what they need or want to tell you, regardless of their speech ability or home language.

An Equal Opportunity Activity

Accessible making and tinkering areas encourage children with a variety of backgrounds and abilities to work and learn together, get to know each other, and share and celebrate their skills and ideas. Making and tinkering activities bring everyone together while also supporting the learning of each child. The possibilities are endless!

Making and Tinkering for All!

Tinkering experiences can be set up to allow for free exploration, with no goal in mind. Making projects might invite children to address a question or solve a problem. All makerspace experiences should be welcoming and inclusive. There are enough possibilities to enable all children to express themselves, share their talents, pursue their interests, and develop their skills and understanding regardless of language differences, cultural backgrounds, and varied abilities.

Read More About It

- *Basics of Supporting Dual Language Learners: An Introduction for Educators of Children from Birth through Age 8*, by Karen N. Nemeth (NAEYC, 2012)
- *The Essentials: Supporting Young Children with Disabilities in the Classroom*, by Pamela Brillante (NAEYC, 2017)
- "Naming the New, Inclusive Early Childhood Education: All Teachers Ready for DECAL!," by Karen N. Nemeth, Pamela Brillante, and Leah J. Mullen (Language Castle, 2015), www.languagecastle.com/2015/08/decalforinclusiveearlyed

---

About the Authors

Karen N. Nemeth is an author, consultant, and Language Castle website host supporting better early childhood education for dual language learners.

Pamela Brillante, EdD, is associate professor of special education at William Paterson University in Wayne, New Jersey. She is a consultant and has worked as a special education teacher and administrator.

naeyc®
Accreditation

This chapter supports the following NAEYC Early Learning Program Accreditation Standards and Topic Areas:

Standard 2: Curriculum
2.A Essential Characteristics
2.J Creative Expression and Appreciation for the Arts

Standard 3: Teaching
3.F Making Learning Meaningful for All Children

Standard 9: Physical Environment
9.A Indoor and Outdoor Equipment, Materials, and Furnishings

CHAPTER 9

Growing Little Storytellers

Ronald F. Ferguson and Tatsha Robertson

When children learn the art of telling stories, it makes them smarter—giving them a head start on success in school and life. They become more aware of the world, and through their stories, they get closer to finding a sense of purpose. They start figuring out what their own roles in the world might be, as human beings. Many preschool teachers encourage children to become storytellers by creating dramatic play centers, sparking pretend play outdoors, and asking children to describe the stories in their artwork.

The power of storytelling is one of the many things we learned while conducting research for our book, *The Formula: Unlocking the Secrets to Raising Highly Successful Children* (2019). While the book focuses on families, we as educators see many ways that the findings are equally applicable to early childhood classrooms.

In the book, we write about smart, highly educated, young leaders who are successful in their professions. Most important, we ask, "What exactly did their parents do to help their children get that way?" We found a pattern in how people raised smart and purposeful human beings, and we call that pattern The Formula.

In our research for the book, we had many long conversations with these young adults and their families about how they were raised. We recognized that successful families inspired a passion for learning in their children, including through teaching storytelling. However, most fascinating of all, we discovered eight types of actions these families took to help their children grow smart and determined to make a difference in the world. We then grouped these parental actions based on the roles the parents played. Many of these roles describe what intentional, innovative preschool teachers do every day.

1. The *early learning partner* plays with the very young child in ways that develop a deep love of learning.

2. The *flight engineer* monitors from afar to ensure things stay on track at school.

3. The *fixer* makes sure that doors to opportunity always remain open to the child.

4. The *revealer* shows the child lots of things to see, do, and be in the world.

5. The *philosopher* answers the child's deep questions about life and respects the child.

6. The *model* sets a good example of how to act and the type of person to be.

7. The *negotiator* prepares the child to get what they want when dealing with powerful people.

8. The *GPS navigational voice* is the parent's voice in the child's head, once the child has left home.

Here, as we focus on storytelling, we also explore the first role, the early learning partner.

You may have heard of Suzanne Malveaux, the television reporter who covered the White House for CNN and has had her own news show. Suzanne's twin sister, Suzette, is very successful too, as a law professor at the University of Colorado. When they were preschoolers, their mother did many things characteristic of early learning partners. She created a home environment that was a storytelling wonderland. It was a launching pad for the skills involved in the jobs Suzanne and Suzette grew up to have, one telling news stories and the other finding the stories in legal cases. In this excerpt from the book, we learn exactly how their mother incorporated storytelling into their play:

> The Malveaux household was a . . . playwriting and storytelling workshop. It was also a library for reading and a stage for both freewheeling and organized play—drawing, singing, puppet shows, and dance. There wasn't anything they could throw away. Why discard an empty toilet paper roll or milk carton when it could be reused to create something fun and beautiful? And a giant refrigerator box was just waiting to be painted and turned into a little house. The girls' favorite project, from age three to early elementary, was creating families out of paper dolls and pasting them on Popsicle sticks. Each family that they created had its own story and look. The dolls represented Asian families, Latin American families, and families that were both black and white. "We would spend hours and hours drawing these little cartoons, and then cutting them out and then storytelling," Suzanne said.

What they didn't know at the time, but maybe their schoolteacher mother did, is that the act of storytelling—of imagining the lives of real people—stretches the brain. Storytellers have to come up with the words their characters will use, the ways they'll move, and even their vocal sounds and emotions. They must imagine how characters will speak with one another and how what one character does will affect what the others will do.

Scientists know that when children tell stories, it helps grow the parts of their brains they need for making plans and working well with other people. Children's chances to be successful when they get older are greater when they expand their ability to remember things, develop the smarts to understand how different parts of their worlds are related to one another (for example, how Mommy's job helps pay for food), and grow the ability to imagine themselves in other people's shoes (learning to be empathetic). Storytelling develops all of these abilities. Helping a child learn to love stories and storytelling is among the most important things early learning partners—including parents, family members, and early childhood educators—can do.

Making Your Classroom a Storytelling Wonderland

When you reflect on how you help children develop storytelling skills, your first thought might be that you do it by reading books to them and asking questions about the characters and events. That's great—the more stories adults read to preschool children, the more able those children are to read their teachers and their friends (i.e., to perceive their thoughts and feelings). This is one of the most important skills a person can develop, and it's a key part of learning to tell stories.

Here are some more ideas for you to try in your classroom—and to share with families—to help children become better and better storytellers.

- Point out objects in the classroom (or home), people in the neighborhood, or plants and weather in nature that children can remember later, giving them raw material for building their own stories.

- Give serious but understandable answers to the questions children ask, using complete sentences and sometimes turning your answers into stories.

- Value children's pretend play and the storytelling that develops. Provide common objects that can become props in their play, like the Malveaux family did using toilet paper rolls, milk cartons, and Popsicle sticks.

- When you read a book aloud, ask children to make up different endings to the story. Invite them to act out the new stories they create!

- Play a game in which you and one child, or a small group of children, take turns adding sentences to a story: You make up a few sentences, then each participant adds sentences, continuing to take turns as the story grows and grows.

- Help each child understand that their own life is also a story and that you and they together have the power to write it—the power to imagine the future and work hard to make it real.

Even in today's world, with smartphones and computers to record our thoughts, storytelling skills that involve thinking and remembering remain much more important than most of us ever imagine. Experts say that telling convincing stories is one way leaders persuade people to work on solving society's most important problems, such as global warming and growing economic inequality. The fact is that we are not just a technological society—we are also a storytelling society.

Many early childhood educators are thoughtful and creative in the ways they help children become great storytellers from their earliest years, including adding storytelling to makerspaces and helping children write and perform their own plays. As teachers know, children have active imaginations! What they need is encouragement and chances to talk with people, to see different places, and to touch things that interest them. All these things can further spark their imaginations while we listen and cheer them along.

About the Authors

Ronald F. Ferguson, PhD, is founder of the Boston Basics and cofounder of Tripod Education Partners. He has taught at Harvard University for 35 years.

Tatsha Robertson is an award-winning multimedia editor and writer with more than 20 years of experience. Her work often focuses on education, early learning, and achievement.

Accreditation

This chapter supports the following NAEYC Early Learning Program Accreditation Standard and Topic Areas:

Standard 2: Curriculum

2.D Language Development

2.J Creative Expression and Appreciation for the Arts

Books that Support Diversity, Conversations, and Play

Shannon B. Wanless and Patricia A. Crawford, with Susan Friedman

Four-year-old Yasmin, who is Black, walks into the dramatic play area, the sound of the beads in her braids clicking to the rhythm of her steps. Her friend Alexis, who is Black, and her teacher, Ms. Cindy, who is White, sit on the floor, talking and choosing beads to put in a doll's braids.

Recognizing this familiar scenario, Yasmin picks up a doll, declares, "I'm Auntie Doreen!," and joins her friend in the play.

Later, Ms. Cindy reads aloud *I Love My Hair!* by Natasha Anastasia Tarpley, and talks about how adults help children take care of their hair. Children share their experiences: "My mother washes my hair every night and dries it with the little blue towel," says Tatiana; "I sit on a chair in the backyard while my grandpa shaves my head," states Delavan. Ms. Cindy repeats that children have different types of hair and that there are different ways adults care for children's hair, but that all of these actions show love.

Ms. Cindy asks the children whether they have noticed that differences in their hair are related to differences in their cultures and ethnicities.

This chapter is adapted from Wanless & Crawford 2016.

Showing children that we see and value all aspects of them—including characteristics related to race, ethnicity, and culture—is a critical step in helping children feel welcome and connected to their teachers and peers. Children's books can serve as jumping-off points to discuss culture, race, and ethnicity and connect to children's play. Here are some great books to read to the children in your classroom.

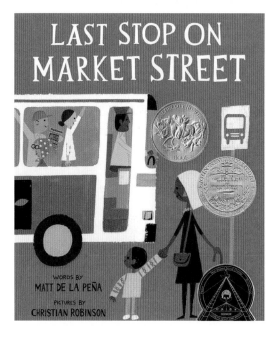

Last Stop on Market Street

By Matt de la Peña
Illustrated by Christian Robinson (2015)

When CJ and his nana ride the bus home, CJ wonders why the street where they get off does not seem as beautiful as some of the others. This book highlights finding beauty in difficult life circumstances. It invites readers to ask questions about economic inequality.

Try This

After the second or third read-aloud, discuss with children what they find most beautiful about their neighborhoods. Then invite them to draw those objects, people, or street scenes.

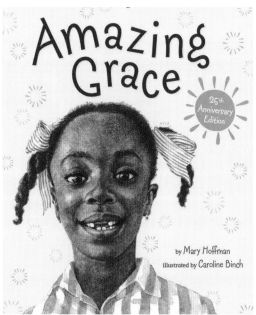

Amazing Grace

By Mary Hoffman
Illustrated by Caroline Binch (1991)

Grace wants to be Peter Pan in the school play, but her classmates tell her she can't because Peter is not Black and is not a girl. The story models ways children can discuss and deal with negative and inaccurate comments related to race.

Try This

Ask children about their favorite stories and characters. Encourage them to use materials from the dramatic play area—or props they create—and pretend to be those characters or act out those stories.

Happy in Our Skin

By Fran Manushkin
Illustrated by Lauren Tobia (2015)

This celebration of skin of every color gives children ideas for how to use positive, descriptive language to describe their own skin color.

Try This

Offer crayons or markers in a variety of hues. Have children draw self-portraits and then describe their skin color.

"More More More," Said the Baby

By Vera B. Williams (1990)

Three vignettes show the loving rituals of children in families of different races. The story invites children to discuss their families' racial backgrounds and how they share love.

Try This

Invite families to visit the classroom and share their histories and traditions. For those who can't come in person, ask if they're able to email photos and descriptions of how their families share love.

About the Authors

Shannon B. Wanless, PhD, is director of the Office of Child Development and associate professor of psychology in education at the University of Pittsburgh. She helps educators use racial literacy and social-emotional teaching practices to improve racial equity and children's sense of psychological safety to learn at school.

Patricia A. Crawford, PhD, is an associate professor in the School of Education at the University of Pittsburgh, where she works in the Early Childhood Education and Language, Literacy, and Culture programs. She is coeditor in chief of *Early Childhood Education Journal*.

Susan Friedman is senior director of publishing and professional learning at NAEYC.

Accreditation

This chapter supports the following NAEYC
Early Learning Program Accreditation
Standard and Topic Areas:

Standard 2: Curriculum
2.E Early Literacy
2.L Social Studies

**Acknowledge and seek to understand
structural inequities and their impact
over time.** Take action when outcomes
vary significantly by social identities (e.g.,
lopsided achievement test scores, number and
frequency of suspensions or expulsions that
disproportionately target African American
and Latino boys, or engagement with certain
materials and activities by gender). Look
deeper at how your expectations, practices,
curriculum, and/or policies may contribute
(perhaps unwittingly) to inequitable outcomes
for children and take steps to change them.

**Develop trusting relationships with children
and nurture relationships among them while
building on their knowledge and skills.**
Embrace children's cultural experiences and
the languages and customs that shape their
learning. Treat each child with respect. Eliminate
language or behavior that is stereotypical,
demeaning, exclusionary, or judgmental.

PART 3

Developing a Strengths-Based Approach When Teaching Black Boys

Every day, educators make choices that benefit some children and families while disadvantaging others. Some of these choices are the result of *implicit bias,* or beliefs and stereotypes that unconsciously affect a person's understanding, actions, and decisions. Implicit biases are associated with different judgment and treatment of children by race, language, gender, ability and disability, body type, physical appearance, and social or economic status—all of which limit children's opportunities to reach their potential. In early childhood settings, implicit bias often impacts young Black boys especially, as is clear in the studies that show the disproportionately high number of Black boys who are suspended and expelled from early childhood education programs throughout the United States as compared with their White peers.

As early childhood educators, it is our ethical responsibility to break down systems of inequity and create learning spaces that support *all* children. The chapters in this section outline considerations for how you can focus on the strengths that Black boys bring to the classroom to best support them and their families, as well as strategies for preventing preschool expulsion.

Read and Reflect

As you read the chapters in this section, consider and evaluate your own classroom practices using these reflection questions.

1. In Chapter 11 (page 67), building strong, reciprocal relationships with families is one of the highlighted strategies to help prevent preschool expulsion, a problem that especially impacts Black boys. Why do you think getting to know a family better might help you to support Black boys in your classroom?

2. After reading Chapter 12 (page 71), reflect on some of your own experiences in relation to Black boys and how teachers perceive their behavior.

3. Chapter 13 (page 77) discusses an expanded definition of school readiness that supports Black boys' frequent desire to be physical. Brainstorm three ways that you can support movement and physicality in your classroom.

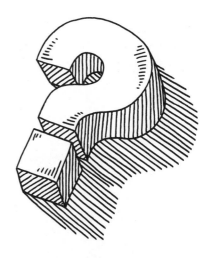

Six Things You Can Do to Prevent Preschool Expulsion

Alissa Mwenelupembe

As a teacher, you strive to support the happiness, health, and development of each child. But as a profession, are we serving all children well? Nationwide, suspension and expulsion from early childhood education programs is prevalent, problematic, and disproportionately impacting Black boys. In state-funded programs, the expulsion rate from prekindergarten is about three times higher than from K–12! While there are many contributing factors, research by Dr. Walter Gilliam and a team at Yale University shows that one important factor is teachers' own implicit biases.

With that in mind, here are six things you can do to prevent preschool expulsion.

1. Consider the Research

Although limited, there is evidence that early childhood educators have implicit biases that affect how they treat children. In Dr. Gilliam's study, both Black and White teachers expected more misbehavior from Black boys than other children. However, Black and White teachers, on average, appeared to differ in the behavioral expectations they held for Black boys, with Black teachers setting a much higher standard.

2. Pause and Reflect

It's natural to think, "I don't do that!" You surely don't do it intentionally. But pause, take a deep breath, and ask yourself hard questions. Self-reflection is a critical step in combating bias. By spending time considering your own experiences and reactions, you can begin to identify your biases. The more you surround yourself with people who think differently or have different experiences, the more flexible your thinking will become.

3. Build Relationships

Ask families about their home routines, the types of celebrations they participate in, the communities they engage with, and their hopes for their children. This information will help you support children's development and provide a foundation for meaningful activities and experiences.

4. Look for Strengths

By focusing on what a child or family knows and can do, you will be able to engage in more positive interactions and have a better sense of how to promote their learning. This will help you build the strong relationships needed to do your best work. It can also foster community and collaboration: as you come to know the families' strengths, you can invite them to the classroom to share their expertise.

5. Speak Out for Equity

When you see things that seem unfair, speak up. If you are not sure where to start, ask questions. What did the child do? Was the child misbehaving, or is there a misunderstanding? What might the child be trying to communicate? How can we support the child and the family? Questions like these can help reframe our thinking and reorient educators and administrators toward what's best for children.

6. Seek Allies

Even if you have to reach out to teachers in other programs or to community organizations, find people who are interested in tackling these issues with you. When we all work together to combat bias, eliminate expulsion, and promote equity, children and families win. As a teacher and a respected professional, you have a responsibility—and a wonderful opportunity—to help challenge and change policies, laws, systems, and institutional practices that keep social inequities in place.

About the Author

Alissa Mwenelupembe has worked in the field of early childhood education for over 18 years as a teacher, coach, director, and college instructor. She serves on the NAEYC National Governing Board.

Accreditation

This chapter supports the following NAEYC Early Learning Program Accreditation Standards and Topic Areas:

Standard 4: Assessment of Child Progress
4.B Using Appropriate Assessment Methods

Standard 6: Staff Competencies, Preparation, and Support
6.D Ongoing Professional Development

Standard 8: Community Relationships
8.C Acting as a Citizen in the Neighborhood and the Early Childhood Community

Black Boys Matter

Cultivating Their Identity, Agency, and Voice

Brian L. Wright

Hakeem, a 4-year-old Black boy, is enrolled at a preschool where most of the staff is White. His parents are proud of their bright-eyed, sweet-tempered, and playful boy. The head of the center, however, finds Hakeem to be "overly aggressive" in the dramatic play and block areas of the classroom.

During the first family-teacher conference of the year, the lead teacher (a White woman with five years of experience) characterizes Hakeem's social and emotional development as "below average" and his intellectual potential as "average at best." Hakeem's parents are confused: Could the teacher be thinking of a different child? Had she really observed Hakeem acting out? What made her think that he was not very bright?

Before the lead teacher responds, the assistant teacher (a Hispanic woman in her first year as an educator) chimes in, sharing an example of Hakeem enthusiastically joining a child who was building a fortress in the block area. When Hakeem accidentally knocked part of it over, he quickly said he was sorry and offered to fix it. "So," says the assistant teacher, "sometimes I think maybe we don't give Hakeem a chance or don't really notice when he does nice things." The assistant teacher folds her arms as she speaks and looks at the ground, appearing nervous about how the lead teacher will react. But her brief comment succeeds in shifting the conversation.

Soon, Hakeem's parents and teachers agree that Hakeem needs more opportunities to play outdoors because he is so energetic. As they talk, the lead teacher admits that his behavior is fairly typical for a child who is in a program for the first time—a key detail she says she had overlooked in her first few weeks working with Hakeem.

Like many other Black families, Hakeem and his parents felt confident enough to question the lead teacher, and the assistant teacher was courageous enough to offer a contrasting opinion. But it's not hard to imagine this situation going another way if the lead teacher had continued to focus on her frustrations with Hakeem's high-energy play rather than acknowledging his enthusiasm and willingness to work with his classmates—leading to a very different outcome for Hakeem.

Black Boys, School Discipline, and Adults' Choices

Throughout the United States, Black boys tend to be viewed as troublemakers from a very young age. Adults often see Black boys as older and less innocent than their White peers (a practice called *adultification*), and their play is perceived as more dangerous, violent, and not developmentally appropriate. According to a 2016 report from the US Department of Education's Office for Civil Rights, Black children make up only 19 percent of preschool enrollment, but they represent 47 percent of preschool children receiving one or more out-of-school suspensions. In comparison, White children represent 41 percent of preschool enrollment but only 28 percent of preschool children receiving one or more out-of-school suspensions. Many of these suspensions are the result of zero-tolerance policies, where even minor "misbehavior," like Hakeem's, triggers automatic penalties that include suspension and expulsion.

Racial disparities in suspension can and do dampen Black boys' enthusiasm toward school—they often get the message that school is a place where they are watched, not welcomed. This in turn makes them less likely to be actively involved in acquiring academic knowledge and skills, socializing with other children, and interacting with teachers. As a result, far too many Black boys are denied genuine opportunities to achieve at high levels because of an unwelcoming classroom climate that contributes to inequity and negative assumptions based on race and gender.

In contrast, culturally competent teachers are aware of the ways Black boys are disproportionately and inappropriately punished in and outside of school. In addition to making sure this wrong is not perpetuated in their classrooms, they seek ways to foster Black boys' developing senses of identity, agency, and voice.

How can teachers learn to identify and address their own biases and increase their cultural competence? How can they best support Black boys' social, emotional, physical, psychological, and intellectual development?

Moving from Deficits to Strengths

Use these questions to prompt your own critical self-reflection as you work to recognize unconscious biases and eliminate them from your classroom.

- Reflect on your perceptions of the children in your class. How might they be affected by the tendency of many adults to view Black boys as older than their actual age and more dangerous than their peers? Ask yourself, "Am I holding the Black boys in my class to different standards of behavior than other children? If so, how?"

- Notice the language you use when talking about Black boys. How often are you using terms like *aggressive, unteachable, hyperactive,* or *out of control*? How does your language shift when you talk about other children?

- Consider how often you focus on what children lack rather than what they bring to the classroom. When reflecting on classroom successes and challenges, try flipping your questions. For example, instead of Hakeem's teacher asking herself, "Why won't that boy behave?," she could have wondered, "What can I do to help turn Hakeem's energy into a leadership opportunity? Would he enjoy leading the class in a game of Simon Says?"

- Pay attention to the activities and materials that most engage the Black boys in your class, and how the children show that engagement. How can you help to nurture these interests and support Black boys' growth (while keeping in mind that not all Black boys will share the same interest in those activities or materials)?

- Learn about the larger structural challenges Black boys face, including the systemic racism that affects family income and wealth, access to resources, representations of African Americans in the media, and the likelihood of involvement in the criminal justice system (which is often summed up as the *school-to-prison pipeline*). Ask yourself, "What obstacles do Black boys face that I haven't acknowledged? How do Black boys reveal their creativity, resilience, resourcefulness, and brilliance in overcoming these challenges?"

When teachers look for Black boys' strengths and reflect on classroom exchanges to try to identify misunderstandings (especially cultural differences), they are more likely to reject stereotypes, build meaningful relationships, and offer the warmth, support, and enrichment that high-quality preschool promises to all children. To ensure that Black boys reach their full potential, it is imperative that teachers proactively take a culturally competent, strengths-based approach. By this, I mean that teaching and learning need to be responsive to the diverse identities of Black boys, including their different languages, literacies, interactional styles, and cultural practices. This cultural responsiveness will help teachers to recognize and engage the positive identity development of Black boys, and to encourage Black boys to use their authentic voices toward agency as full and respected community members.

From Reflection to Action

A few weeks after their initial meeting, the lead teacher reaches out to Hakeem's parents again. She has been reflecting on her assumptions, biases, and practices, and realizes that she has a long way to go to become the culturally competent teacher she wants to be.

During the meeting, his teacher shares that she is starting to understand Hakeem's behavior from his parents' perspective. Most days, he is more easily excitable, energetic, and verbally expressive than the other children. But now that she is looking for Hakeem's strengths, the lead teacher also sees that he is more engaged, enthusiastic, and encouraging toward his classmates than the other children.

Hakeem's parents appreciate that the lead teacher is trying to learn and grow. They spend a while discussing his interests. The lead teacher is surprised to hear of Hakeem's fascination with modern dance. His parents say it started with the family going to see a live performance and later enrolling Hakeem in classes at a community dance studio. Since Hakeem's time in dance, he has taught his family modern dance techniques. His interest in modern dance has continued through his parents reading a dozen books to him from their local library about modern dance and Alvin Ailey American Dance Theater. His teacher, who grew up taking dance classes, leaves the meeting brimming with ideas for projects Hakeem might want to pursue to learn more about modern dance.

Reflecting on the meeting, the lead teacher comes to another important realization: her surprise at Hakeem's curiosity about modern dance was a sign of an assumption about what boys in general are "supposed" to be interested in, and Black boys in particular. Taking her next step toward cultural competence, Hakeem's teacher realizes that she needs to avoid a "one size fits all" perspective based on stereotypes about Black boys, their interests, and the ways they learn and interact with others.

Conclusion

When teachers spend time reflecting on themselves and their practices and then turn those observations into concrete change in the classroom, they enable Black boys to bring their own experiences, ideas, and practices into the learning space as important and enriching contributions.

In Chapter 13 (page 77), I provide suggestions for activities and practices that can help Black boys feel like valued members of the classroom community (rather than troublemakers) and that create space for Black boys to thrive.

About the Author

Brian L. Wright, PhD, is assistant professor and coordinator of the early childhood education program at the University of Memphis. For a more thorough exploration of how teachers can nurture the Black boys in their classes, see *The Brilliance of Black Boys: Cultivating School Success in the Early Grades,* with contributions by Shelly L. Counsell, which won the National Association for Multicultural Education's 2018 Phillip C. Chinn Book Award.

Photographs: pp. 70, 72, 73, 74, courtesy of Shelby County Schools Division of Early Childhood Education and the Barbara K. Lipman Early Childhood School and Research Institute at the University of Memphis

naeyc®
Accreditation

This chapter supports the following NAEYC Early Learning Program Accreditation Standards and Topic Areas:

Standard 2: Curriculum
2.L Social Studies

Standard 6: Staff Competencies, Preparation, and Support
6.D Ongoing Professional Development

Standard 7: Families
7.A Knowing and Understanding the Program's Families
7.B Sharing Information Between Staff and Families

Black Boys Matter

Strategies for a Culturally Responsive Classroom

Brian L. Wright

In American classrooms—including preschool classrooms—studies show that Black boys are more likely to be seen as "problem" children than their peers, and they are less likely to be considered ready for school. For example, a Yale Child Center study found that preschool teachers spent more time watching Black children than White children when looking for disruptive behaviors. Proactive, culturally competent teachers can work to counter these misperceptions and create classroom environments where Black boys feel welcome to learn, dream, and be themselves.

In Chapter 12 (page 71), I focused on how teachers can identify and begin addressing unconscious biases about Black boys through self-reflection. Here, I offer teachers practical suggestions to help them foster Black boys' positive identity development, promote agency and voice, and create conditions that will empower Black boys to succeed in school.

A Culturally Responsive, Strengths-Based Approach

It is important that teachers focus on what Black boys know, understand, and can do as opposed to what they do not know, do not understand, or cannot do. Culturally responsive, strengths-based teachers do not engage Black boys from a deficit perspective (i.e., having "problems to fix" or being "at risk"). Instead, they seek to learn about Black boys' strengths, gifts, and talents.

Three ways teachers can take this approach are by tapping into the power of history, celebrating Black boys in books, and rethinking school readiness.

Tapping into the Power of History

Culturally responsive teachers work to affirm Black boys' experiences through the content of their lesson plans. They incorporate books, visuals, and other materials that reflect Black histories, lives, and points of view.

For example, many preschool teachers use the concept of "history and me," which celebrates the richness of African American history and the roles Black boys and men have played in bringing about social change through taking a stand for social justice and equity. When teachers embed a "history and me" perspective within the social studies curriculum, they also create opportunities to emphasize current examples of Black boys and men as valuable community members.

This kind of exposure is critical to the boys' development of a healthy sense of self and agency. Learning about the important discoveries and courageous acts of Black boys and men from the past and present can serve as an important reminder for today's Black boys to see themselves and their communities as vital parts of American history. It also empowers them to challenge the "troublemaker" and "bad boy" stereotypes found in typical portrayals of Black boys.

Reading and discussing carefully selected picture books is a great way to incorporate "history and me" into preschool classrooms. For example, the biographical account *Richard Wright and the Library Card*, written by William Miller, and historical fiction such as *Sit-In: How Four Friends Stood Up by Sitting Down*, written by Andrea Davis Pinkney, show Black boys how young people like them have accomplished great things.

Preaching to the Chickens: The Story of Young John Lewis, written by Jabari Asim, is another great real-life story. It shows how John Lewis—long before he became a Freedom Rider and US congressional representative—used play to imagine and then act out his dream of becoming a preacher and inspiring people to improve their lives. In addition to reading aloud *Preaching to the Chickens* and discussing Lewis's life, teachers may want to add materials to their dramatic play centers to help children imagine and act out their dreams.

Other books to consider for developing a "history and me" approach include *Freedom Summer*, written by Deborah Wiles, and *Delivering Justice: W.W. Law and the Fight for Civil Rights*, written by Jim Haskins. Both show young African American men using their agency to challenge racial discrimination in the South.

Although the focus of this chapter is Black boys, it's worth noting that seeing the accomplishments of Black men and boys through these stories also helps children from different racial and ethnic groups. Through a thoughtfully planned read-aloud, critical discussions, and related classroom activities, all children can come to understand that the cultural stereotypes they may have absorbed about Black boys are myths.

Celebrating Black Boys in Books

Much like history and social studies books, carefully selected, authentic multicultural children's books can also introduce Black boys to mentors on paper. Black boys, perhaps more than any other group of children, need access to what Rudine Sims Bishop calls "mirror" books—books that reflect themselves, their families, and their communities in positive ways. Currently, there are far more "window" books—books that give Black children a glimpse into the lives of other people (mainly the White world)—than mirror books showing their own communities. These mirror books highlight cultural histories, music, the arts, language varieties, fashion, cuisine, and other culturally rich experiences found in Black communities to engage Black boys.

Here are some picture books that feature Black boys facing the kinds of situations children might see in their everyday lives.

- In *Riley Knows He Can* and *Riley Can Be Anything,* written by Davina Hamilton, Riley first overcomes his stage fright to play a wise king in the class play and then imagines the many possible careers he might have.

- Derrick Barnes's *Crown: An Ode to the Fresh Cut* celebrates the Black barbershop as a place that can transform a boy into the stylish king of his neighborhood.

- Combining the "history and me" and mirror approaches, *Hey Black Child*, written by Useni Eugene Perkins, and *Dad, Who Will I Be?,* written by G. Todd Taylor, use words and visuals to introduce readers to important people and events from African American history and encourage Black boys to pursue their dreams.

Seeing characters like themselves in these books can help Black boys develop a stronger sense of themselves, including their abilities to pursue their goals and tell their own stories.

Rethinking School Readiness

Culturally responsive classrooms honor and value the cultural and personal identities of all children, and Black boys in particular. One area in which this can be challenging is typical measures of readiness for kindergarten. Teachers can avoid the effects of unconscious biases by taking a strengths-based approach to readiness.

One common indicator of kindergarten readiness is how long a child can sit quietly in a classroom. Sustained periods of quiet sitting may be helpful from a classroom management perspective, but they do not reflect what we know about the importance of movement in learning. In addition, long periods of quiet sitting undermine children's verve. The term *verve* is often used to describe energy and spirit in the arts; in education, it refers to having high levels of energy—being physically active and "loud"—when mentally stimulated. Verve is a great description of how many Black boys behave when they are excited about learning. With the concept of verve in mind, culturally responsive teachers can encourage indoor and outdoor large motor and whole body experiences, such as by putting mats in spacious areas to encourage Black boys—and all children—to tumble and roll.

Another common indicator of readiness is how well children follow rules. The ability to meet school and classroom expectations is considered good behavior. While following rules can ensure safety and help children understand what is expected in a particular setting, teachers should consider whether the rules are stifling children's expressive individualism. Black boys, and other children, benefit from being creative and taking risks as they explore, experiment, and follow where their curiosity leads them. Knowing this, culturally responsive teachers are flexible in the ways they interpret "good behavior." They reflect on children's reasons for not following rules and create opportunities for spontaneous, ongoing exploration of "What if . . . ?" questions.

Culturally responsive, strengths-based teachers also consider the implicit bias of some kindergarten readiness indicators like obeying instructions without questioning or challenging authority figures (compliant behavior). This expectation of quiet obedience clashes with the oral cultural practices of many African Americans; it may also hinder their pursuit of fairness,

equity, and consistency in their education. A blunt and direct communication style may be perceived by some teachers as rude or a sign of a "bad" or "disrespectful" child. In contrast, culturally responsive teachers acknowledge children's cultural heritages as legacies that affect dispositions and attitudes. These teachers understand that Black boys' questions are indications of engagement, curiosity, and brilliance that are worthy of addressing in the classroom.

Conclusion

As with all children, the social and emotional well-being of Black boys must be our highest priority. Making sure we see them, hear them, and know them is the starting place for providing them with schooling that is humane, culturally responsive, equitable, and strengths-based. Culturally responsive practices and strategies, like those discussed here, support and promote Black boys' positive identity development, agency, and voice inside and outside of school. This is what we should strive for as early childhood education professionals. Our Black boys matter, and they need, want, and deserve nothing less.

About the Author

Brian L. Wright, PhD, is assistant professor and coordinator of the early childhood education program at the University of Memphis. He is author of *The Brilliance of Black Boys: Cultivating School Success in the Early Grades,* with contributions by Shelly L. Counsell, which won the National Association for Multicultural Education's 2018 Phillip C. Chinn Book Award.

Photographs: pp. 76, 78, 80, 81, courtesy of Shelby County Schools Division of Early Childhood Education and the Barbara K. Lipman Early Childhood School and Research Institute at the University of Memphis

naeyc®
Accreditation

This chapter supports the following NAEYC Early Learning Program Accreditation Standard and Topic Areas:

Standard 2: Curriculum
2.E Early Literacy
2.L Social Studies

Communicate the value of multilingualism to all families. All children benefit from the social and cognitive advantages of multilingualism and multiliteracy. Make sure families of emergent bilinguals understand the academic benefits and the significance of supporting their child's home language as English is introduced through the early childhood program, to ensure their children develop into fully bilingual and biliterate adults.

Design and implement learning activities using language(s) that the children understand. Support the development of children's first languages while simultaneously promoting proficiency in English. Similarly, recognize and support dialectal differences as children gain proficiency in the Standard Academic English they are expected to use in school.

Supporting Emergent
Bilingual Children

Research shows there are many benefits to growing up learning more than one language, including increased cognitive flexibility (the ability to adapt quickly to changing situations). With over 22 percent of children in the United States speaking a home language other than English, teachers are more likely than ever to have emergent bilingual learners (also known as dual language learners) in their classrooms (Kids Count 2018; Zeigler & Camarota 2018). This can be challenging, especially when there are multiple home languages. Many teachers need concrete strategies they can use to support children's language development in both English and their home languages as well as children's learning in content areas like math and science.

Emergent bilingual children and their families bring valuable knowledge and many different gifts and strengths into your classroom that can enhance the learning experiences of all children. The chapters in this section outline effective strategies for teaching emerging bilinguals and for welcoming and engaging families who speak languages other than English.

Read and Reflect

As you read the chapters in this section, consider and evaluate your own classroom practices using these reflection questions.

1. Which practices described in Chapter 14 (page 85) are already in place in your classroom? What are some ways they have positively impacted children's learning? Pick one new strategy to try. How do you think it will support the learning and inclusion of all children?

2. It's ideal when teachers also speak the home language of the children they teach, but in superdiverse classrooms, that's unlikely to be the case. Do you use any of the environmental supports described in Chapter 15 (page 91) to promote conversation and interaction among the children? If not, select at least one to try. What are the results?

3. How does the strategy of previewing materials and concepts in children's home languages before new material is introduced, as described in Chapter 16 (page 97), support equitable learning for all children?

4. Have you ever done a story walk before? Practice with a colleague and then try it with the children you teach. What book did you use? What illustrations or concepts did you focus on as children and families identified phrases in their languages to use with the book? What were the results?

Supporting Emergent Bilingual Children

A Checklist for Early Childhood Educators

Shelley Pasnik and Naomi Hupert

More than ever, early learning settings serve children who are growing up with more than one language in the home and at school (children known as *emergent bilinguals* or *dual language learners*). Research shows that learning multiple languages is very beneficial for children's development. This checklist will help you support young children's bilingual learning in a rich literacy and language classroom environment.

This chapter is adapted from EDC 2019b.

Promising Practices

We reviewed current research to find the most promising practices for you to use in supporting emergent bilinguals in your classroom whether you're a new teacher or a veteran, whether you have one emergent bilingual child or many, whether or not you use a dual language model, and whether or not you speak the home languages of the children in your classroom.

We found three main areas of focus for helping these children thrive in your classroom and for laying the foundation for success in speaking multiple languages in later grades:

- Supporting children's use of their home languages
- Valuing children's home cultures
- Using specific teaching strategies to help children be successful

Practical strategies in each of these areas are outlined in the checklist. For more detailed information, see the companion guide, *Supporting Emergent Bilingual Children in Early Learning.* Both resources are available for free in English, Spanish, and Simplified Chinese at www.edc.org /early-ed-tools.

You can use this checklist at any time—but we think it's especially useful at the beginning of the school year, as you prepare your classroom to welcome children who are emergent bilinguals. You also can review this checklist in collaboration with the other teachers in your classroom and in your school or center.

Keep in mind that it may not be practical to apply every checklist item in all classrooms. You know your children and your classroom best; use your judgment to choose what to incorporate into your classroom.

For materials in the children's home languages, you may need translation help from school staff, a parent volunteer, or a community member who knows the language, or you can use a translation website.

Overall Classroom Environment

☐ **Labels are used selectively throughout the classroom,** located at children's eye level, in large print, and in the languages of the children to help children connect text and language to real objects and to lay a foundation for language and literacy development. Labels can be made initially for high-frequency or commonly used vocabulary words, such as *the* or *red,* and new words can be added gradually throughout the year. Each language can be color coded.

☐ **Directions for actions, routines, and schedules are posted** for children, with a short, clear line of text and a clear image. Examples include an illustrated job chart, an image of hands being washed posted above the sink, and a picture of the sun on a calendar to show the weather for that day.

☐ **Images and text reflecting different cultures and languages** are visible to children, such as a calendar of multicultural holidays, maps, flags, and photos of places and people in traditional clothing. You can highlight the cultures and languages of the children in these displays.

☐ **Rotating themes and key words are introduced regularly.** Themes such as Animals and Community Helpers are used often throughout the classroom and in class activities to promote vocabulary development in English and in the children's languages.

☐ **Photos and objects relating to the children, their families, and their cultures are included throughout the room.** You might post photos of each child dressed in the traditional clothing of their culture, with the names of the clothing underneath in English and in the home language, and have a "family shelf" where different children share objects from their home lives and cultures each week. You also can post children's work and label it in their home languages as well as in English.

☐ **Families are made to feel welcome through a bulletin board,** which greets them, invites their participation, and gives them class updates—in their home languages, if possible.

Learning Centers in Your Classroom

☐ **The reading center includes storybooks and informational books that are easy for young children to follow,** with pictures, rhymes, and repetition.
- Include books in different languages—especially in the children's home languages—and bilingual books, when possible
- Include books from different cultures, not just translations of books written in English

☐ **The writing center includes easily accessible writing materials,** such as pencils, crayons, markers, paper in different sizes and colors, foam letters, alphabet strips, and other items.
- Include cards with the names of the children in your classroom and other high-frequency words in children's home languages and in English
- Incorporate materials that include the alphabets of children's home languages and other written materials in the home languages, if possible

☐ **The math center includes books, math words, math games, and manipulatives in English and in children's home languages.** For example, hang posters showing numbers from 1 to 10 in English, Spanish, or other languages spoken by the children.

☐ **The science center includes hands-on science learning materials.** Examples include leaves collected by students and child-friendly equipment like hand lenses, as well as books and labels in English and in children's home languages.

- Place art materials in the science center so children can express what they learn and observe about science in various ways, such as through drawings, collages, gestures, and talking

☐ **Play areas include items from different cultures and in different languages.** Here are some examples:

- Dress-up clothes from different cultures
- Dolls and puppets that are culturally, ethnically, and racially diverse and that combat stereotypes, such as female firefighters and Black scientists
- Board games in various languages

Classroom Materials and Resources

☐ **Art materials are multicultural.** Here are some examples:

- Activities and materials from different countries/cultures, such as origami paper with traditional prints or materials to make traditional masks from the children's cultures
- People-shaped paper, along with crayons, markers, and colored pencils in a range of skin tones
- Labels for materials and colors in English and in the children's home languages

☐ **Music materials include instruments, photos, and recordings of music, songs, and dances from various cultures,** such as maracas and photos of folk dancers. These can be labeled in English and in the children's home languages.

☐ **Technology and media resources are used to support development in English and in children's home languages.**

- Child-to-child conversations can be supported by pairing children to use media resources, with appropriate seating and headphone splitters, if necessary
- Media resources, such as apps, videos, poems, songs, and stories, have content available in children's home languages
- Devices can record and share audio, video, and pictures of children's home cultures and languages

☐ **Meals include ingredients and snacks from multiple cultures.** You also can invite families to bring in food from their cultures for birthdays, holidays, and other celebrations, if your school or center allows it.

Where to Learn More

- For detailed guidelines for creating a literacy-rich classroom environment: **Learning Words for Life** www.ncbi.nlm.nih.gov/pmc/articles/PMC4612362

- For a classroom model of working with young emergent bilingual children and their families: **The Early Years: Dual Language Learners** https://wida.wisc.edu/sites/default/files/resource/FocusOn-EY-Dual-Language -Learners.pdf

- For a summary of general characteristics of young emergent bilingual children and essential instructional practices: **Working with Young English Language Learners: Some Considerations** www.ericdigests.org/2004-2/young.html

- For a pre-K–12 English language learners guide with forms to track children's language development (reading, fluency, comprehension, etc.) and common classroom phrases in Spanish and cognates: **ELL Starter Kit for Educators** www.colorincolorado.org/guide/ell-starter-kit-educators

- For articles written by teachers and researchers on welcoming and supporting emergent bilingual children: **NAEYC's Topic Page: "Dual Language Learners"** NAEYC.org/resources/topics/dual-language-learners

About the Authors

Shelley Pasnik leads early childhood initiatives at the Education Development Center (EDC), a global nonprofit that works on behalf of young children and the adults in their lives in more than 80 countries.

Naomi Hupert codirects the Center for Children and Technology at EDC, which has spent the last 60 years actively defining and supporting inclusive education practices.

Accreditation

This chapter supports the following NAEYC Early Learning Program Accreditation Standards and Topic Areas:

Standard 2: Curriculum
2.A Essential Characteristics

Standard 3: Teaching
3.A Designing Enriched Learning Environments

Standard 9: Physical Environment
9.A Indoor and Outdoor Equipment, Materials, and Furnishings

Standard 10: Leadership and Management
10.E Personnel Policies

Many Languages, One Classroom

Supporting Children in Superdiverse Settings

Carola Oliva-Olson, Linda M. Espinosa, Whit Hayslip,
and Elizabeth S. Magruder

> Matthew, a monolingual English speaker, and two assistants who speak Spanish
> and Tagalog, teach in a classroom with children who speak five different home
> languages. The classroom buzzes with new songs and phrases in English and
> sometimes words of comfort in each language. Carefully placed pictures
> and labels help children see and interact with key words and items from all
> their cultures. In one corner of the classroom, Matthew welcomes a new parent
> and arranges a family language and cultural background interview.

Note: Chapters 15 and 16 build on the article "Many Languages, One Teacher: Supporting Language and Literacy
Development for Preschool Dual Language Learners," by Elizabeth S. Magruder, Whitcomb W. Hayslip,
Linda M. Espinosa, and Carola Matera, which appeared in the March 2013 issue of *Young Children*. Based on
feedback received from teachers, the authors expanded the strategies described there to more fully support
young dual language learners in attaining the benefits of full bilingualism.

Two Classroom Language Models

In schools across the United States, many teachers who try to help children become bilingual use one of these two language models. Both work well with our POLL strategies. This chapter elaborates on the second one.

The Fifty-Fifty Dual Language Model

Teachers make sure children experience (e.g., hear, speak, see in print) both English and their home language in all content areas, such as literacy, math, and outdoor play. With careful planning, teachers ensure that children experience equal exposure to both languages and also provide a clear structure for language separation.

This is a great model for supporting emergent bilingual children, but it is most feasible when all of the children speak the same home language (e.g., Spanish). Two different home languages can also be supported in this model through careful allocation of time and other instructional resources. (For an example of a classroom that embraces English, Spanish, and Arabic, see Chapter 18 on page 111.)

The English Language Development with Home Language Support Model

Teachers most often use this model when they are not proficient in the children's home languages. It gives them a clear and consistent plan for when and how to use English and when and how to use the children's languages. Children learn mainly in English during instructional time, but benefit from home language and multicultural supports that teachers intentionally interweave throughout the daily routine. For a description of specific supports to use, see the POLL strategies described in this chapter.

Are you one of the many teachers today with children in their classrooms who speak a number of different languages and are just beginning to learn English? Teaching in a classroom like this is a challenge! How in the world do you go about it?

You need concrete strategies you can use to support children's language development in both English and their home languages. Of course, it's ideal when teachers speak the children's languages. But in superdiverse classrooms, that's unlikely to be the case.

Here, we offer strategies from an approach we call *personalized oral language learning* (POLL). Teachers who have tried them find these strategies especially useful for supporting the learning and development of children in classrooms with a range of languages.

Personalized Oral Language Learning

As centers and schools serve more and more children who speak little or no English at home—and as we recognize the many benefits of children retaining their home languages and cultures—teachers often ask us, "What are the specific strategies I should use to support my dual language learners?" POLL answers this question with three types of assistance: (1) family engagement, (2) environmental supports, and (3) conversation and interaction. In this chapter, we address the first two strategies. Chapter 16 (page 97) explores strategies for fostering conversations and interactions with children who are dual language learners.

Family Engagement

Start by gathering information about each child's experience in the home language and in English. This is a critical step. We highly recommend that you meet with families in a personal, face-to-face interview to collect this information—along with information about the family's background and their shared interests and activities. (For a sample interview about family languages and interests, see page 94.) A personal meeting is much more effective than sending home a questionnaire or having an informal conversation. This is not the only time for the teaching team to meet with families, but it's the beginning of a relationship and dialogue focused on the importance of both home language and English language development.

Through this type of teacher–family collaboration, you can plan together how to weave linguistic and cultural information into activities at school and at home. For example, families can have conversations with their children in their home languages on the topics/themes and new words shared by the teachers each week. Interviews and ongoing communication also provide perfect opportunities for you to invite parents and other family members to volunteer in the classroom!

As the school year progresses, be sure to keep families involved in the classroom's storybooks, themes, and learning concepts. Communicate with them in the languages they are most comfortable speaking (you may need to use an interpreter). Try reaching out in different ways, such as frequently sending home two-way journals for families to read, write in, and return; having regular small-group coffee chats with parents before the school day; emailing, texting, and holding frequent casual conversations at pickup and drop-off; and scheduling one-on-one conversations. Your reminders will reinforce families' awareness of the importance and benefits of their using the home language in everyday activities, having rich conversations with their children, reading, telling stories, and playing.

> The home languages of the children in Ding's family child care program include Spanish, English, and Vietnamese. Ding's home language is Vietnamese, and she speaks English fluently.
>
> Ding knows that one child's family owns a food truck. She has invited the family to park the truck outside her home one morning to share food items with the children and show them steps the family takes in preparing and selling food. Ding plans vocabulary activities based on food prices and menus from each child's culture. She chooses related books in all three languages and prepares materials for the children to use in creating a food truck in the dramatic play area.

Environmental Supports

When you create a warm, nurturing environment, one that welcomes children and families, you send the message that you value and respect them, their language, and their culture. When your classroom includes the home languages and cultural backgrounds of all the children and families, they see and feel that they are natural and important parts of classroom activities. You'll soon notice positive results: young dual language learners will develop confidence, communicate their thoughts and feelings more readily, concentrate better, and learn more.

Transform your classroom into a rich setting with areas for children to talk and play, and with spaces for both quiet and active learning and small group interactions. Here are some supports to use:

- Label in each of the home languages of the children, with one color for each language used consistently throughout the classroom for schedules and topic displays. (Use an online translation tool, like Google Translate, and ask parents to help with specific words.)

Family Languages and Interests Interview

Child's Name: _____ **Date:**_____
(first, middle, last)

Child's Date of Birth: _____/_____/_____
(month)   (day)   (year)

1. Who are the members of your family that your child interacts with regularly? _____

_____

2. Are there other people (not family members) who live with you and your child? If yes, what language(s) do they most often speak to you child? _____

3. Who is the primary caregiver of your child? _____

4. What language(s) does the primary caregiver speak most often with child? _____

5. What language(s) did your child learn when he or she first began to talk? _____

6. Can you tell me what language(s) each of the following people in your household speak to your child?

	Only English	Mostly English, plus another language (identify)	Mostly another language (identify), some English	Only another language (identify)
Mother (or you)				
Father (or you)				
Grandmother/ Grandfather				
Primary caregiver other than parents				
Others, such as siblings and cousins				

7. Are there activities in the community where your child interacts with others who speak your home language?

_____

8. What special talents or interests does your child have? _____

9. What kinds of stories does your child enjoy? _____

10. Who does your child play with most often and what language do they speak? _____

11. What are your hopes and dreams for your child? _____

12. What are your expectations for your child for the coming year? _____

13. Do you have any hobbies or interests that you would like to share with your child's class? _____

_____

14. Would you be interested in volunteering in your child's class? _____

- Place environmental print in all the children's home languages—everyday objects like magazines, food packaging, and commercial products—throughout play areas and the classroom.
- Display family photos, books, artifacts, and posters and other visuals from all the children's cultural backgrounds throughout the classroom at child's-eye level and in learning centers. Families are often eager to help supply the classroom with items from their home that represent family and cultural traditions, such as examples of artwork, empty food boxes, and pictures.

Teachers can work with librarians to select books in the children's languages that relate to curricular themes and can adapt puzzles to include writing in all the children's languages. Families can share songs, rhymes, and *dichos* (playful sayings) in all the languages of the children; they can also help stock the dramatic play area and art center with clothing and cultural artifacts from each child's background.

Conclusion

Without a doubt, fostering young dual language learners' development of English and also of their home languages is a major challenge. But if you use the strategies outlined in this chapter, you can partner with families and create a responsive environment that supports each child and encourages learning.

About the Authors

Carola (Matera) Oliva-Olson is associate professor at California State University Channel Islands. She supports dual language programs and offers professional development as an independent consultant.

Linda M. Espinosa, an emeritus professor of early childhood education at the University of Missouri, Columbia, was a co-principal investigator for the Center for Early Care and Education Research–Dual Language Learners at the Frank Porter Graham Child Development Institute, the University of North Carolina at Chapel Hill.

Whit Hayslip served as the assistant superintendent for early childhood education in the Los Angeles Unified School District and currently consults for the David and Lucile Packard Foundation.

Elizabeth S. Magruder, a senior program associate at WestEd's Center for Child and Family Studies, supports dual language professional development as an independent consultant.

Photograph: p. 90, courtesy of Betsy Nikolchev

Accreditation

This chapter supports the following NAEYC Early Learning Program Accreditation Standard and Topic Areas:

Standard 3: Teaching
3.B Creating Caring Communities for Learning
3.F Making Learning Meaningful for All Children

More Strategies for Supporting Children in Superdiverse Settings

Carola Oliva-Olson, Linda M. Espinosa, Whit Hayslip, and Elizabeth S. Magruder

All across the country, teachers welcome to their classrooms children who speak a number of different languages and are just beginning to learn English. In these superdiverse classrooms, teachers need strategies to ensure the children experience *personalized oral language learning* (POLL).

Personalized Oral Language Learning

In Chapter 15 (page 91), we provided POLL strategies for engaging families of young dual language learners and enriching the classroom environment with examples of the children's languages and cultures. Here, we offer POLL strategies for fostering conversations and interactions with children.

Conversation and Interaction

Keep in mind that it's really important for children to see, hear, and speak their home languages throughout the day. They need to see books and environmental print in their languages all through the classroom. They should hear teachers use key words and phrases in their home languages, even when the teachers don't speak the languages well—or at all!

All teachers can learn a few phrases in each child's home language to say hello and goodbye, ask children how they are feeling, and generally engage with them—for example, *please* and *thank you*, praise, encouragement, directions, and expressions of interest and surprise. The children also need opportunities to speak their home languages in conversations with fluent adults, say, family or community volunteers or staff members.

Using children's home languages for behavior management and emotional support seems to come most easily. But don't forget to ensure the languages are used intentionally for instructional purposes, like previewing and reviewing new concepts and key vocabulary words before introducing them in English. (These are activities that parents and volunteers can carry out.) Teaching in this way will improve dual language learners' comprehension of lessons presented in English, increase their ability to learn important preschool concepts, and help them bridge what they know in their home languages and what they need to learn in English.

Key Strategies to Try

Preview materials and concepts in children's home languages, when possible:

- Write and explain *intentional messages*—
these help children to understand the purpose
of each lesson or learning experience, and
they incorporate content vocabulary.

**Use new English vocabulary throughout
the day and across all domains:**

- Represent new vocabulary in multiple ways—
pictures/photographs, diagrams, physical gestures,
movement, drawings, etc.
- Schedule daily vocabulary activities in groups of no
more than three to five children. They may include
neighborhood walks, mealtime conversations, and
targeted daily times focused on language activities.
- Lead the class in fun theme- and vocabulary-related
chants, songs, and poems.
- Avoid simultaneously translating during instruction.
- Accept children's language mixing—that is, their
code switching.

Add a translation step to your instructional planning:

- Find fluent volunteers or use an online translation tool (like Google Translate), and practice
the pronunciation of vocabulary in other languages.
- Ask the children to help translate and to teach key words for everyone to learn. This
communicates the value of learning multiple languages. It also lets children feel pride
in their home languages!

Try to provide fluent models for each home language:

- Invite volunteers and family and community members who are fluent in the children's
languages to lead reading circles for new storybooks and to have informal conversations
with children.

**Read aloud books in English multiple times to give children several opportunities to
understand and enjoy the story:**

- Encourage the children to act out stories using English during repeated interactive readings.
- Lead a story walk (that is, flip through the book's pages and illustrations and highlight key
parts of the story) using words and phrases gathered from the children and their families in
their home languages.

Manraj, a native Punjabi speaker fluent in English, is an assistant preschool teacher in a multilingual classroom. He selects *Little Owl Lost,* by Chris Haughton, for its short text and its simple but interesting vocabulary that aligns with the children's English language skills. He asks all the families to use and talk in their own languages about the key words from the book.

Later, Manraj takes a small group of five children on a story walk through the book. He holds up the book, reads the title, points to the cover picture, and asks, "What is an owl?" When no one answers, he asks, "I wonder what the word for *owl* is in Spanish? Or in Vietnamese?" Pablo whispers, "*Tecolote,*" and Ahn calls out, "*Chim cú!*" Manraj responds, "Yes, *owl* means *chim cú* in Vietnamese and *tecolote* in Spanish. Let's all repeat: *owl.*" He continues in the same way with key words on the rest of the preselected pages.

Hold a daily dialogue with each child to stimulate frequent story-centered conversations, using questions at the child's language level. Offer prompts to support the child's responses, and accept mixed language use.

- Build on a child's responses using more complex grammar and unusual words in a way that follows and expands the child's interest and curiosity.
- Use repetitive phrases and use materials such as props, photographs, and illustrations to encourage peer-to-peer story retelling and the sequencing of essential plot elements in English. See an example of this strategy in action—children using a felt board—in this video: https://bit.ly/2PMESf6.

Plan the curriculum based on thematic units that immerse children in specific, related topics so they have time to grasp essential concepts and internalize and use key vocabulary.

- Use intentional messages, as you did in the preview, to reinforce the unit's big ideas and key vocabulary.
- Schedule daily vocabulary activities during center time, neighborhood walks, and mealtime conversations, in small groups of no more than three to five children, using gestures, props, and photographs to convey meaning.

> The teacher hears a child sharing that his uncle is coming to visit this week from Colombia. He is flying in a large airplane for many hours. The teacher asks the child to share his news with the group. Later she notices the children building airplanes in the block area. She develops a lesson focused on airplanes and displays the following intentional message: *Airplanes are powerful machines.*

Conclusion

When you apply the POLL strategies as field-tested steps that lead to overall language development, you turn children's home languages into tools for learning (rather than obstacles to learning). Meeting the needs of dual language learners in superdiverse preschool settings becomes a welcome opportunity to promote activities and interactions that raise the quality of learning for all children!

About the Authors

Carola (Matera) Oliva-Olson is associate professor at California State University Channel Islands. She supports dual language programs and offers professional development as an independent consultant.

Linda M. Espinosa, an emeritus professor of early childhood education at the University of Missouri, Columbia, was a co-principal investigator for the Center for Early Care and Education Research–Dual Language Learners at the Frank Porter Graham Child Development Institute, the University of North Carolina at Chapel Hill.

Whit Hayslip served as the assistant superintendent for early childhood education in the Los Angeles Unified School District and currently consults for the David and Lucile Packard Foundation.

Elizabeth S. Magruder, a senior program associate at WestEd's Center for Child and Family Studies, supports dual language professional development as an independent consultant.

Photographs: p. 96, © Getty Images; pp. 98, 99, 100, courtesy of Carola Oliva-Olson

Accreditation

This chapter supports the following NAEYC Early Learning Program Accreditation Standard and Topic Areas:

Standard 3: Teaching
3.B Creating Caring Communities for Learning
3.F Making Learning Meaningful for All Children

Embrace the primary role of families in children's development and learning.
Recognize and acknowledge family members based on how families define their members and their roles. Seek to learn about and honor each family's child-rearing values, languages (including dialects), and culture. Gather information about the hopes and expectations families have for their children's behavior, learning, and development so that you can support their goals.

Uphold every family's right to make decisions for and with their children. If a family's desire appears to conflict with your professional knowledge or presents an ethical dilemma, work with the family to learn more, identify common goals, and strive to establish mutually acceptable strategies.

Engaging
Diverse Families

There are times when, as an educator, you may have conflicting opinions with families about how to best support children's learning and development. How do you share your perspective while also acknowledging that families bring essential knowledge and perspectives to your work with their children? It all comes down to reciprocal relationships. But what does it mean to have reciprocal relationships with families?

To advance equity, a family must be recognized as the best experts about their child—their relationship with their child began before you met and will continue long after their child leaves your classroom. You can do this in a number of ways, including honoring a family's right to make decisions for and with their child, taking time to get to know and build relationships with the children and families you work with, offering a variety of ways for each family to get involved based on the level of engagement and collaboration they are able to offer while maintaining high expectations for family involvement, and seeking and using information from families to inform the curriculum you develop, the classroom materials you provide, and the interactions you have with children. The following chapters explore strategies you can implement and resources you can use to forge reciprocal relationships with the families of the children you teach. Building these strong connections is at the core of supporting children. When you embrace a family's strengths and contributions, beautiful things can happen in your classroom!

Read and Reflect

As you read the chapters in this section, consider and evaluate your own classroom practices using these reflection questions.

1. In Chapter 17 (page 107), the author shares a special experience she has with a child during a home visit and how it leads to a stronger connection between them in the classroom. What strategies from the chapter do you think would be helpful to incorporate in your own home visits? If your program does not support or provide you with the resources for home visits, which practices might you embed in the classroom setting instead and how?

2. When you don't share a culture or language with a child, it can sometimes feel hard to connect with her. Brainstorm some open-ended questions you might use to start a meaningful conversation with a child or family from a different culture, like those featured Chapter 18 (page 111).

3. After reading Chapter 19 (page 117), consider some of the forms you have families fill out or holidays your class celebrates. What adjustments could you implement to help all children and families feel welcome and included?

4. Chapters 18 and 19 both highlight that inviting children to share stories about their families is a great way to help everyone feel welcome in the classroom. Why do you think giving children opportunities to tell authentic stories about their own families is so important? How do you or can you incorporate children sharing stories about their families into your daily classroom routine?

5. Meaningful, enriching math experiences at home and school contribute to children's long-term educational outcomes, and Chapter 20 (page 119) provides four ways you can support families in helping their children learn math. How do you think enriching children's math experiences at home and school connects with equity?

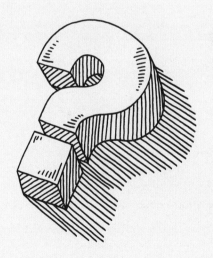

Photograph: p. 104, © Getty Images

Knock, Knock . . . Who's There?

The Benefits of Home Visits in the Early Years

Jennifer K. Lampe

My first visit to Aamiina's home is something I'll never forget. When I knock on the door, I am greeted by the whole family, who smile and welcome me inside. In the living room, we all sit on the floor to eat and talk about our lives, about the family's hopes for Aamiina in her new classroom, and, of course, about the food we're eating!

I learn that in Somali culture, people eat only with their hands. They believe that if the food touches a utensil, the spirit that lives within the nourishment the food provides is broken. Unsure whether I will be comfortable eating with my hands, Aamiina's mother offers me a spoon. I politely decline, scoop up a bite of okra in my hand, and continue talking with the family. I leave their home feeling like I know Aamiina and her family. I can't wait for the school year to begin.

On the first day of school, Aamiina walks into the classroom and says good-bye to her *hoya* (mom) without a single tear. She comes right over to me, and we begin to play.

Whether it's a child's first school experience or simply his first time in a new school or class, having a friendly face in the classroom on the first day of school helps him know that he's safe. Home visits are a great way to encourage children and their families in these transitions. Spending time getting to know a child's family outside of school shows the family that you care about them and that they can trust you with one of the most important people in their lives. And when children see the adults they trust opening their door to you, they learn that you're safe too.

In meeting with children and their families, the goal is to help them feel comfortable in the first few days of school—and beyond. For families who are new to the community or the country, like Aamiina's, the home visit can be especially helpful. It may be the child's first experience entering school in a new country, and she—and her family—may feel overwhelmed by the prospect of starting school in a place where they don't have a shared language or cultural identity. If children and families have a chance to get to know you before that first day, you can assist them in feeling like a vital and respected part of the learning community you'll be building together over the coming year.

Planning Your Home Visits

Home visits go much more smoothly when you enter them feeling prepared! A few weeks before your program starts, spend some time thinking through your goals for the visits and planning how you can accomplish them.

Call families on the phone. Phone calls are more personal—and more likely to get responses—than emails or text messages. It might be helpful to write out a script of what you'd like to say. Try something like this:

> Hi, this is Jenny Lampe from the Child Development Center. I'm calling to introduce myself and share how excited I am to have you and your child in Room One with me this upcoming school year! If you're open to it, I'd like to set up a time where I can meet with you so we can get to know each other.

Have a backup plan. While most families are open to meeting at their homes, it may not be welcome or possible for all of them. Make a list of public spaces, like parks, libraries, or community centers, where you can meet instead. Your goal is to build a relationship, and that can be accomplished in any setting where you can spend time together.

Bring supplies (not paperwork). Have a pad of paper on hand so you can jot down a few notes during your conversations with families or immediately after the visit (before you forget important details). Your notes will help you integrate some of the things you learn about them and their child into your classroom. Try to avoid bringing lots of forms for families to fill out.

Create some magic. If possible, select a few classroom materials that children and their families can play with and enjoy. A "magic bag" full of fun, interactive materials reinforces the message that you're in the family's home to get to know them. Reintroducing these tools and materials during the first week of school helps children make connections between their home visit and classroom experiences. Here are some possibilities:

- Children's books
- Puzzles
- Art materials
- Pipe cleaners and beads to string on them
- Windup toys
- Colorful buttons, pom-poms, or other small objects to sort

During Your Visit

The key to a successful home visit—one that helps you become not just a familiar face but a welcome one—is conversation. When you spend time getting to know children and their families, you help the family see you as more than just a hello at drop-off in the morning and then again at pickup in the afternoon. Each conversation will be different because each family is different, but there are several common threads.

Ask questions—and listen to the answers. Ask families about their day, their summer, or their well-being—anything other than school (see "Conversation Starters" on page 110). Allow the conversation to build as you and the family get to know one another as people outside the classroom, but with the common interest of helping their child thrive.

Engage with children at their speed. The young children of the family will be watching you to see what you do—where you sit, how you talk with their family members, and how you approach them. Sit on the floor (if possible) to make yourself accessible, and wait for the children to approach you as they're ready. Have your magic bag close by and ready to share.

> Aamiina's first morning in our class flies by. Before I know it, it's time for lunch. Aamiina's family has packed all her favorite foods, many of which we enjoyed together at their home. I don't put a spoon next to her lunch, and I hope this will help Aamiina feel comfortable when she comes to the community table—but when she does, she will not eat.

Conversation Starters

Ideally, conversations should develop organically so that families don't feel like they're being quizzed—but it's also nice to have a few questions in your back pocket if you get nervous or aren't sure what to talk about next. If you get stuck, the following questions may help you come to understand what's important to your families:

- What tools or materials is your child drawn to?
- What does your child call you?
- What kinds of interests have you noticed your child has?
- Is your child afraid of anything?
- What activities do you like to do as a family?
- What does a typical weekend look like for your family?
- What's something you'd like me to know about your child?
- What are some regular household routines your child is a part of?
- What do you think we can do at school to make your child feel included?

I try talking with her, offering my hand to help her eat, and pretending to eat her lunch with her to share in the nourishment, but none of these things work. At the end of the day, I talk to her family, but they also have a hard time figuring out why Aamiina chose not to eat.

Later that night, I think back to my time in Aamiina's home and my conversation with her family—how we gathered on the floor in the living room to share our food and our stories. And then I realize what I've been missing.

The next day, I ask Aamiina if she would like to sit on a blanket with me while we eat lunch. She smiles, joins me, and happily begins to eat. When the other children ask why we're sitting on the floor, I tell them it's because it helps Aamiina feel safe in our classroom. Some of the children ask if they can join us on the blanket, and we all talk about the things that help us feel safe.

Home visits are the first step in building relationships with children and their families that will make your classroom a warm, supportive community. When children feel safe, they learn and explore more freely—and they're more likely to share their needs and express their feelings and ideas with you and with their classmates. A few weeks into the school year, after having eaten lunch on the blanket with me every day, Aamiina opted to join her classmates at the table for the first time!

About the Author

Jennifer K. Lampe, MEd, is a lead toddler teacher at the Kent State University Child Development Center in Kent, Ohio.

Photographs: pp. 106, 108, © Getty Images

Accreditation

This chapter supports the following NAEYC Early Learning Program Accreditation Standard and Topic Areas:

Standard 7: Families
7.A Knowing and Understanding the Program's Families
7.B Sharing Information Between Staff and Families

Conversations with Children!

Asking Questions to Support Their Understanding of Family Diversity

Janis Strasser

When we ask children questions—especially big, open-ended questions—we support their language development and critical thinking skills. By encouraging them to tell us about themselves—their families, home languages, and traditions—we show our respect for their unique family and cultural perspectives and their funds of knowledge.

Using an adaptation of Bloom's Taxonomy to think about the types of questions to ask, I've listened to teachers' conversations with children to explore how different types of questions invite meaningful conversations and create new learning opportunities.

For this chapter, I visited an ethnically diverse preschool classroom of 4-year-olds, housed in a large, urban elementary school in New Jersey. The families of the 15 children in the class originally came from a variety of Spanish- and Arabic-speaking countries. Ten children were bilingual, speaking both English and their home language well. The other five were emergent bilinguals just beginning to learn English. In addition, three children had special needs. One teacher was a native Arabic speaker and the other a native Spanish speaker. The talk among children and adults was in English, Spanish, and Arabic. The books and labels around the classroom were in English, Spanish, and Arabic as well.

What Are Funds of Knowledge?

Children come to school with unique blends of background knowledge and experiences. These are rooted in their home languages, family and community cultures, everyday activities, and significant events. They are children's funds of knowledge.

Learning about and appreciating children's and families' funds of knowledge helps teachers in many ways—forming strong relationships, identifying children's strengths, enriching the classroom community, and planning engaging activities.

To learn more about funds of knowledge and how they support early childhood education, watch this video from Head Start: https://eclkc.ohs.acf.hhs.gov/video/funds-knowledge-video

Morning Meeting

Morning meeting starts with the teachers drumming and chanting "Good morning" in English, Spanish *(Buenos días)*, and Arabic *(Sabah al-khair)*. They ask each child, individually, "How are you?" in the language the child is most comfortable with. This question focuses on understanding—by asking it, the teachers show they value children's individual responses and their home languages. Throughout the day, activities presented to the whole class are usually in English, but discussions continue in all three languages.

The morning I visited, the teachers did a read-aloud of Vera B. Williams's picture book, *"More More More," Said the Baby*. The book describes the unique ways three different families show their love for their young children. When the story is finished, the teachers invite children to share their own family stories and traditions by asking different types of questions that meet the needs of the children in the class.

"How is your family the same as or different from the families in the story?" **(Analyze)**

The children talk about their siblings and relatives and compare the sizes of their families. To expand the conversation, the teachers remind them of a project they worked on earlier in the year, when they made a graph representing the number of people in their families.

Each and Every Child

The questions "Who is your favorite person in your family? Why?" **(Evaluate)** move the conversation in a different direction as one child describes his mom. A different boy mentions a big sister who plays cards with him. Another child describes a relative who takes her shopping. The teachers smoothly integrate English, Spanish, and Arabic throughout the morning meeting, making comments like "Tell me more!" or "What else?" to encourage children to expand their responses.

Two Different Follow-Up Conversations, Two Different Topics

The teachers talk with children individually and in small groups to continue conversations that began during morning meeting. They ask open-ended questions, letting the children guide the conversation based on their responses and interests.

Conversation About Cooking and Family Recipes

Ms. Hamdah: Tell us about your family. **(Understand/Describe)**

Lina: Mommy love to cook.

Ms. Hamdah: Tell us about what she cooks. **(Understand/Describe)**

Lina: *Shatah.* (*Several children nod their heads and smile as the teacher explains that this is an Arabic hot sauce—like ketchup but spicy.*)

Ms. Hamdah: If you were the chef in your house, what would you cook? **(Apply/Relate to)**

Zander: *Freekeh.* (*Again, several children agree and the teacher explains that this is a grain dish.*) I help mom with milk and lemon.

Cruz: *Mi abuela,* she cook the rice and I like it.

Ms. Hamdah: Can you tell us how it tastes and how she cooks it? **(Understand)**

Cruz: No. I, no. I like it.

Ms. Hamdah: I wonder how your abuela's rice is the same as and different from the freekeh. **(Analyze/Compare)**

Ms. Hamdah: Let's ask your families about the ingredients they use and how they cook the foods you described. Let's write letters to your families with these questions. **(Create)** Once we have their answers, we will compare the recipes and share opinions on these foods you love. **(Analyze and Evaluate)**

Understanding Different Types of Questions

Bloom's Taxonomy has long been used as a way to think about the types of questions we ask students. We have adapted it for young children. Although *Remember* has mostly right or wrong one-word answers and *Create* invites use of the imagination and answers that are complex and unique to each child, these levels are just guides. It is up to you to consider which types of questions are appropriate for each child you work with. The lower levels form the foundation for the higher ones.

Remember
identify, name, count, repeat, recall

Understand
describe, discuss, explain, summarize

Apply
explain why, dramatize, identify with/relate to

Analyze
recognize change, experiment, infer, compare, contrast

Evaluate
express opinion, judge, defend/criticize

Create
make, construct, design, author

Later, in the dramatic play center, the teacher asks Zander to share more about how he helps his mom cook. He talks about *sebanik* (spinach) and *labneh* (similar to yogurt). They have several back-and-forth exchanges about cooking chicken. He says it is his favorite because it is "super-duper good."

Looking at a menu from a local restaurant, the teacher asks, "If you made your own menu with the foods you like from home, what would you put on your menu?" **(Apply)** "Maybe you could make your own special menu in the art area and we could add it to the dramatic play center." **(Create, if the child decides to do so.)**

What High-Level Questions Aren't—and What They Are

A high-level question is *never* a yes-or-no question ("Do you have a pet?") or a question that has an obvious answer ("How many wheels does that car have?"). Nor is it a question that has only one answer ("How old are you?"). The answers to those kinds of questions demonstrate that children understand language, are paying attention, and can count or identify numbers, colors, or shapes—but the questions don't give children opportunities to think deeply.

A high-level question is *always* a question that each child will answer in her own way. This shows that she is using what she knows and what she's learning instead of just recalling information. There's an easy way to tell if a question is effective—a child will be excited to give you lots of details in her answer.

(From Strasser & Bresson 2017)

Conversation About Travel and Where Families Live

Ms. Luna: When taking a trip, where does your family like to go? **(Understand/Describe)**

Nina: We go to Mexico.

Antonio: We go to Canada.

Ms. Luna: What can you tell us about these places? **(Remember and Understand/Describe)**

The children start talking among themselves.

Abbas: I have house in my country [Jordan].

Ms. Hamdah: How does it look different than your house in New Jersey? **(Analyze)**

Abbas: It looks really old but it never break. It is made of bricks.

Ms. Hamdah: Tell us how it looks when you walk into it. (*He hesitates.*) Close your eyes and remember. **(Remember and Understand/Describe)**

Abbas: There is a living room. It has TV that puts on *Theater Jenna*. There is a kitchen and *betagin*.

The teacher explains to the other children in the group that the word means *eggplant*. Believing that Abbas has much more to say but does not yet know the words in English, she continues the conversation in Arabic for a few minutes.

Switching back to English, the teacher explains that two of the biggest differences between his homes in Jordan and New Jersey are that he has a patio and an attic in Jordan. Abbas nods enthusiastically. She adds that *Theater Jenna* is a religious program on TV.

Supporting Conversations About Families

- Look for opportunities to provide experiences where children can appreciate their individual and group identities.

- Include classroom materials (books, art, dolls) that represent people from diverse racial, cultural, and linguistic backgrounds.
- Create a wall of family photos to help children see that there is diversity within families, cultures, and linguistic groups.
- Balance diversity with connectedness by pointing out both similarities and differences across shared experiences, like celebrating birthdays.
- Invite children to create class books about families (including things like favorite activities and special relatives). These can be placed in the library area for everyone to explore and return to over time.

Things to Remember When Engaging in Conversations with Dual Language Learners

- If a child in your class speaks a language you don't speak, find a colleague, another adult, or another child who can participate in conversations in that child's home language.
- Understand that the child may feel shy about responding in English.
- Use gestures, pictures, and labels to help the child understand.
- Allow extra time for the child to respond.
- Ask the child's family to help you learn some words, phrases, and questions in the home language (Nemeth 2012).

Conclusion

Asking questions about families offers opportunities for children to express complex thoughts. In their answers, children describe and analyze how their families share many commonalities and at the same time have their own unique traditions. These engaging conversations also help children learn about their peers' families, cultures, and languages as they develop an appreciation for diversity.

Note: Thank you, master teacher Dalia, for suggesting that I visit Ms. Hamdah and Ms. Luna's classroom. A big hug to all of the wonderful children who patiently helped me learn lots of new words in Spanish and Arabic, sang, and told me all about their families. Karen Nemeth, your tips for working with dual language learners have provided such good insights!

About the Author

Janis Strasser, EdD, is an early childhood teacher educator, author, and consultant. She recently retired from William Paterson University, where she was a professor of early childhood education for 20 years. She has worked in the early childhood field for 45 years—during the first 15, she was a preschool and kindergarten teacher.

Photograph: p. 112, courtesy of the author

NAEYC
Accreditation

This chapter supports the following NAEYC Early Learning Program Accreditation Standard and Topic Area:

Standard 3: Teaching
3.F Making Learning Meaningful for All Children

When I Have a Mommy and a Mama

Including Children with All Types of Family Structures in the Classroom

Julia Luckenbill

Every year, you work hard to set up your classroom for the incoming children and their families. You select a range of books and decorations that reflect the children, try hard to learn their families' names, and tailor the activities to the children's abilities and interests. But this year is different. Maybe it's the first time you've ever had a child with two mommies, or a dad but no mom, or a grandparent as guardian. Excited about the start of the school year—and a little nervous about accidentally saying the wrong thing—you want to prepare so that all of the children and their families feel welcome in your classroom.

Here are some tips for your journey:

- **Ask family members (including all primary caregivers) what they prefer to be called.** You can collect this information during home visits, at your program's open house, or through intake forms. Make sure to take note of and use the names they prefer, such as abba, papa, and grammy, in future communications.

- **Revise all forms and handouts so family members can easily write in their title(s) (e.g., father, mother, parent, guardian, grandmother) and preferred pronouns.** Try to use correct pronouns.

- **Invite each child to bring in a family photo and display all the pictures in your classroom.** Encourage children to take turns sharing stories about their families and photos. Validate their family stories with positive comments that show you value the differences in families, like having one parent or being adopted.

- **Listen carefully to children's questions and comments about families,** especially in the first several weeks of the school year. You can set the tone for inclusion and excitement about different family structures by being intentional in how you respond to the children.

- **Think of the children and families you work with and adjust planned themes and activities for holidays** like Mother's Day or Father's Day to celebrate "Family Day" so all families are included. Be sure there are supplies available for those children who want to make more than one gift or card on a key day. Provide support for children leading up to and on key days when they have to navigate not having a father or mother.

- **Consider the language on cards for families.** For example, "You are the sweetest mom," may cause a child with two mothers to worry which mother will get the card. Try something open ended like "My family is special because . . ." The more children can personalize the language, the more appropriate the card can be, especially if the family member identifies as a different title than mother or father.

- **Advocate for children in social interactions and listen closely for teachable moments.** When families are different, peers may have lots of questions or comments.

- **Continue to invite the children to share about family members throughout the school year.** Comments like "My dads took me to the pumpkin patch" or "My granny had a birthday" create opportunities for the children to learn from each other, with your support. Giving children space and encouragement to share stories about their families shows you respect and value all of the children and families in your program.

About the Author

Julia Luckenbill, MA, is the program coordinator for the infant–toddler program at the NAEYC-accredited Early Childhood Laboratory School at the University of California, Davis, Center for Child and Family Studies. She is also a child development demonstration lecturer.

Photograph: p. 116, © Getty Images

naeyc ®
Accreditation
™

This chapter supports the following NAEYC Early Learning Program Accreditation Standards and Topic Areas:

Standard 1: Relationships
1.A Building Positive Relationships Between Teachers and Families

Standard 2: Curriculum
2.L Social Studies

Standard 3: Teaching
3.B Creating Caring Communities for Learning

Standard 7: Families
7.A Knowing and Understanding the Program's Families

Advancing Equity

Playful Ways to Extend Math Learning at Home

Jessica Mercer Young and Kristen E. Reed

Some things are essential to young children's healthy development—things like caring relationships, plenty of time to play, and enriching environments, to name just a few. If you were filling out this list of essentials, would frequent opportunities to learn math make your top 10? We hope so!

This chapter is adapted from EDC 2019a.

Several studies have reported that early math skills are a strong predictor of later academic performance. In fact, math knowledge and skills in kindergarten are related to later math, science, and even reading skills. This is true regardless of gender, race, or family income.

Unfortunately, not all children have equal opportunities to engage with math concepts at home or in preschool settings. Children from underresourced communities tend to start kindergarten with less math knowledge than their more advantaged peers. While this opportunity gap starts before kindergarten, it extends all the way to the college years. Yet there is no better way to close this opportunity gap than by providing high-quality early childhood education.

Mastering Math: Make Math Playful!

Giving young children lots of meaningful and enriching math experiences, both in school and at home, can build a firm foundation for later math learning—and contribute to advancing equity in children's long-term educational outcomes.

The Home–School Connection

Schools often advise families to read to their children every night. Shared book reading fosters children's language and literacy skills, builds vocabulary, and instills a lifelong love of reading. We think it's critical to give families a similar message about shared math experiences at home.

At first, many families may balk at the notion of doing math activities. Maybe their own math experiences were tense. Or maybe they don't know what kind of math is right for young children or how to make math playful.

But we've seen that with teachers' encouragement and guidance, families love engaging in math activities with their children. They find great joy in doing problem-solving games and puzzles, singing songs, and reading books that build children's early math skills!

Children naturally engage in mathematical ways of thinking. For example, they look for patterns, classify, compare, and count as part of making sense of the world. With support from caregivers—that is, interactions with teachers, family members, and other important adults in their lives—these math-based ways of exploring the world can be extended to support school readiness skills like problem solving, puzzling, and perseverance.

Four Ways to Support Family Math

1. At back-to-school night and during family–teacher conferences, talk about doing fun math activities at home and how they reinforce children's math learning in school.

2. Remember that it's important for children to explore and to feel safe making mistakes. Having the freedom to make mistakes actually supports learning. Tell families about how much adults' positive attitudes toward making mistakes—and toward math, in general!—matter. (See "Tips for Families" on page 125).

3. Share "Fun, Easy Ways to Play with Math at Home" (pp. 124–125) with families. It offers ideas for fun family math activities—and multiple opportunities for children to practice thinking mathematically. Post it on your class bulletin board and put it in materials that you send home. Families might not even realize that some of their favorite activities involve math!

4. Select math games for children to play in the classroom and at home. See the samples we share in "Math Games for School and Home" (pp. 122–123)—these are part of our free eight-page math mini-book series. (Templates and instructions are available at www.ym.edc .org/math-books/mini-books.) At the end of each mini-book, there is a short activity for families to do together. There's also a note for families about the key math concepts featured in the book and why they are important for young children's mathematics learning.

Math Games for School and Home

One effective strategy is to teach children a math game in the classroom and then send the game home for them to play with their families. Children are proud to share something they learned in school and to teach it to others. And families have a chance to learn more about what is happening in the classroom.

Visit www.ym.edc.org to find math mini-books (for teachers and families) with games on many math topics—shapes, numbers, patterns, and more—in both English and Spanish. The games are adaptable and are meant to be played again and again. Children's sophistication in game play—and in mathematical understanding—will increase over time. The simple explanations and notes that accompany the games help families build their own confidence in math and their understanding of how to help their children learn math.

How old are you?
¿Cuantos años tienes?
by Kristen Reed & Jessica Young
Book/Libro 4c
5
Name/Nombre_____

How Many Are Hiding?
¿Cuántos Se Están Escondiendo?
by Kristen Reed & Jessica Young
Book/Libro 6
Name/Nombre_____

I hid some of my pennies! How many pennies do you see? How many are hiding?

¡Escondí algunos de mis centavos! ¿Cuántas centavos puedes ver? ¿Cuántas están escondidas?

Are you this age?
¿Tienes tú esta edad?

w many pennies do you see?
Cuántos centavos puedes ver?

I have 3 pennies in all.
Tengo 3 centavos en total.

About the Authors

Jessica Mercer Young is a senior research scientist and developmental and educational psychologist specializing in early learning at the Education Development Center (EDC) in Waltham, Massachusetts.

Kristen E. Reed is a senior project director and mathematics educator at EDC.

Photographs: pp. 120, 123, courtesy of EDC; p. 124, © Getty Images

naeyc®
Accreditation

This chapter supports the following NAEYC
Early Learning Program Accreditation
Standard and Topic Areas:

Standard 2: Curriculum

2.B Social and Emotional Development

2.F Early Mathematics

Fun, Easy Ways to Play with Math at Home

Jessica Mercer Young and Kristen E. Reed

Did you know that some of your favorite family activities involve math? It's true! Here are just a few ideas for how you can get your child to build her math thinking skills at home.

1. **Sing songs and chant!** Many songs, chants, and verses have patterns. Learning a song's pattern helps children remember the song. Patterns *repeat in a predictable way that helps children know what comes next*. Songs and chants, like "Five Green and Speckled Frogs," "Five Little Monkeys," "Hokey Pokey," and "Ten Little Fingers," teach number order—children count up or down from a number. They also teach spatial words, like *on*, *in*, *out*, and *around*.

2. **Read picture books.** Visit your local library and check out great picture books about counting, numbers, patterns, measurement, shapes, and engineering. For ideas, take a look at the book lists at www.ym.edc.org/math-books/published-books and https://earlymath .erikson.edu/series/book-ideas.

Adapted from *Games for Young Mathematicians*, a program of research in early mathematics at the Education Development Center, supported by funding from the National Science Foundation and Heising-Simons Foundation. For more math information and games, visit www.ym.edc.org.

3. **Use your fingers.** When children count on their fingers, they are strengthening their number knowledge and their ability to visualize numbers in their minds. You and your child can play these two games with fingers, toys, and other objects—or even people!

   - **How Many Do You See?** Have your child count your fingers and see how many different ways you can "show 5" on two hands. Then, you can show numbers up to 10. Eventually, add your child's hands and go up to 20.

   - **How Many Are Hiding?** Start with your whole hand and "hide" some fingers. Ask children, "How many fingers are hiding?"

4. **Do puzzles.** Playing with puzzles helps children to think about spatial relationships, identify shapes, look for patterns, and find solutions. Start with easy jigsaw puzzles and add more challenging ones when your child is ready. You can even make your own puzzles by drawing a picture and cutting it into two, three, four, or more pieces!

5. **Build together.** Building with materials like blocks, cardboard boxes, LEGO bricks, K'Nex, Magna-Tiles, or Lincoln Logs helps children develop strong spatial skills.

6. **Try origami.** The creations children make by folding paper help them develop strong spatial skills as well as logical and sequential thinking. In addition to being art, origami can be found in packaging all around us—pizza boxes, paper bags, envelopes, and take-out containers. Folding (and unfolding) paper helps children think in two and three dimensions and see how the sequence of steps affects the final design.

7. **Play board games.** While playing games like Candy Land, Chutes and Ladders, Hi Ho Cherry-O, and Sorry, children move a game piece one space at a time while counting the number of spaces (an important math skill). Your child will practice recognizing the numbers of dots showing on the die without counting them. She'll also develop perseverance, engage in problem solving, and learn from mistakes.

8. **Play card games.** Games like Memory, Go Fish, War, Slap Jack, Crazy Eights, Uno, and Sleeping Queens give children practice in recognizing and comparing numbers. They also help children learn to pay attention to things like shape, number, and color.

Tips for Families

- Mistakes are okay! Making mistakes is a part of learning new things. When your child makes a mistake, ask questions like "What happened?" and "What would you do differently next time?" to help him see it, and talk about what he can learn from the experience.

- Children tend to mimic parents' attitudes about math. As you play these games, have fun! If you are having fun, they will too! Working through a challenge is also what makes games enjoyable. It's no fun to play a game that's too easy. If things get tough, you can remind children that sometimes math makes us think hard, but that challenges are good for our brains.

Adapted from *Games for Young Mathematicians*, a program of research in early mathematics at the Education Development Center, supported by funding from the National Science Foundation and Heising-Simons Foundation. For more math information and games, visit www.ym.edc.org.

Recommendations from
the Position Statement

Actively promote children's agency. Provide
each child with opportunities for rich, engaging
play and opportunities to make choices in
planning and carrying out activities. Use open-
ended activities that encourage children to work
together and solve problems to support learning
across all areas of development and curriculum.

**Speak out against unfair policies or practices
and challenge biased perspectives.** Work to
embed fair and equitable approaches in all
aspects of early childhood program delivery,
including standards, assessments, curriculum,
and personnel practices.

**Look for ways to work collectively with others
who are committed to equity.** Consider it a
professional responsibility to help challenge and
change policies, laws, systems, and institutional
practices that keep social inequities in place.

Exploring Identity,
Fairness, and
Activism

You strive to create a learning environment where young children feel safe to explore complex feelings and topics, but talking about identity, differences, and fairness can feel tricky. You might wonder how to give children space to explore their thinking and ideas about diversity if you're uncomfortable or anxious talking about it yourself. Or you may be unsure how to guide children as they talk about the racial and cultural differences they notice among themselves. The chapters in this section offer guidance from a number of educators about supporting children's healthy identity development and teaching children about fairness and valuing human differences.

As important as your work is in the classroom to help children learn about fairness and equity, early childhood educators alone cannot resolve issues of fairness and equity in our society. The position statement on equity says that teachers have an obligation to be advocates for children, families, and the profession. Some educators find this daunting, while others eagerly embrace this role. How can you move from teaching with an equity lens in your classroom to advocating for equity on a larger scale? There is no one way to start. At the end of this section, you can read about one educator's journey from teacher to advocate.

Each and Every Child

Read and Reflect

As you read the chapters in this section, consider and evaluate your own classroom practices using these reflection questions.

1. What is your comfort level when children talk about their differences? The author of Chapter 21 (page 131) shares that she wants to listen closely to uncover children's points of view and misunderstandings. How does listening closely to children's exploratory conversations about identity support their identity development?

2. Chapter 22 (page 137) describes children's emerging thoughts on gender and fairness as they contemplate the imagery on bathroom signs. What reactions did you have to the children's discussions about gender and fairness? Why?

3. In Chapter 23 (page 143), the author describes how she needed to clarify information about segregation to her preschoolers after they read the book *Martin Luther King, Jr. and You*. Have you ever had to explain a complex historical topic to young children? The chapter also includes a number of reflection questions that the author asked herself. As you've thought about your own teaching, have you ever asked yourself any of these questions? What questions could you add?

4. After reading Chapters 10 (page 61) and 23, consider the books on your bookshelf. Are any of them nonfiction books? How many of them explore science topics or historical events? How do reading and discussing interesting nonfiction books that build children's content knowledge support equity?

5. Chapter 24 (page 149) suggests that talking to a trusted colleague or friend to discuss your struggles and passions can help you clarify what you most care about and why. Have you ever had one of these conversations? If not, consider who you might have this discussion with. What topics would you choose to discuss?

6. A great way to begin advocating for young children is to recognize your own biases. Project Implicit has created a number of research-based implicit association tests (https://implicit.harvard.edu/implicit/takeatest.html) that you can take to identify and better understand your attitudes and beliefs on various topics, including race, religion, and sexuality. Take one of these tests and write a reflection about the results. If you're comfortable doing so, coordinate taking one of the tests with a trusted colleague so that each of you can take turns sharing and discussing your results.

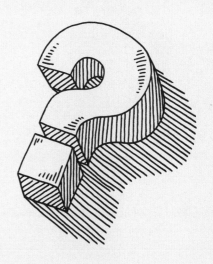

Photograph: p. 128, © Getty Images

"What If I Say the Wrong Thing?"

Talking About Identity with Young Children

Nadia Jaboneta, with Deb Curtis

One day during lunch, a few children engaged in a conversation about their identities. This inspired other children at the table to think and share more about themselves and ask me about myself too:

Christina: I'm half Indian and half vegetarian.

Matthew: You know you best, Christina! I'm half Jamaican.

Christina: What's your other half, Matthew?

Matthew: Oh, I don't know. I'm gonna find out.

Anjali: I'm half Indian too! Zade, you're Indian too, right?

Zade: No, I'm from Michigan. I'm American.

Willem: I'm Chinese . . . I think.

Gavin: Me too, Willem. I think I'm part Indian too.

Ronin: My mom is half Japanese, my dad is half Japanese, and I'm half Japanese.

Riku: I'm half Japanese too! What are you, Nadia?

Nadia: I'm Peruvian. Our conversation reminds me of a book that teacher Tiffany shared with me about how people are the same and different. We can read it after lunch, if you like!

Meals are a special time in my classroom. While we are enjoying a family-style lunch, conversations naturally emerge: daily, the children initiate and engage in dialogue about topics such as family structure, religion, race, ethnicity, gender identity, and gender expression. Here are some snippets of conversations I have heard:

- "Just because I like sparkly things does not mean that I am a girl. Boys can like sparkly things too!"
- "I have a mom and a birth dad."
- "Me and my mom have different skin color, and that's okay."
- "I believe in Jesus and God; who do you believe in?"

Conversations like these can be sensitive and difficult because there are so many biases related to being different, and often we have been taught to avoid talking about differences. In my experience, adults often shy away from discussing these topics, especially with young children. In fact, in the past I have redirected many of these conversations because I felt uncomfortable or unsure of how to respond. I thought, "What if I say the wrong thing?"

Nadia's Reflections

I now realize I don't always need to have an answer. Instead, I should take up the challenging task of becoming an anti-bias educator. This means I must confront my own biases and be willing to feel uncomfortable as I negotiate my role in children's identity development and understanding of others.

Children form beliefs about themselves and others by watching and listening to the important adults in their lives. I want to be a teacher who listens closely to uncover children's points of view and misunderstandings. If I avoided these sometimes uncomfortable conversations, what message would I be sending to the children? They may think that it's not okay to ask questions about differences or to share their thinking about topics such as race, ethnicity, religion, gender identity, and family structure. In fact, research shows that children develop prejudices when topics such as race are avoided.

It's important to me that children know they are in a safe place where they can share who they truly are, what they believe in, and what they wonder about. It's crucial that they be heard and feel validated and important.

The children remind me how significant these real talks can be. I have come to expect these types of conversations and want to be ready to respond when children share their stories. I often wonder what conversations are happening (or are not happening) at home. Some children have misunderstandings about their identity; what is my role when children's stories reflect inaccuracies? Should I correct them?

Before I offer the children information, I follow their lead and try my best to honestly explore what they're thinking about. I let them know I'm there to listen to their ideas. If children are scared, I assure them that I am there to keep them safe. If children are confused, I help them think about their questions and make a plan to find out more about what they want to know. If children show biases in their conversations, I help them think about how their words may be hurtful and unfair.

Reflective Questions

Use the following questions from the Thinking Lens to reflect alone or with a colleague.

Know Yourself

- What is your response to the children's conversation? What is your experience and comfort level with talking about identity—including topics such as skin color, race, and religion—with children? Have you ever worried that you might say something wrong?

- As an early childhood professional, what values and beliefs do you have about your role in furthering children's understanding of these complex issues and in guiding their development to value diversity?

- How would you assess your knowledge and skills in supporting children's identity development and appreciation of differences? Are you interested in developing more skills and knowledge to engage in these kinds of conversations, as Nadia describes?

Find Details of Children's Competence

- What examples of the children's strengths and competencies do you hear in their conversation? What is valuable about the way the children talk about their similarities and differences?

- How can capturing details of children's conversations support you in understanding and responding to their thinking?

Seek Children's Points of View

- What is each child's perspective on his or her identity? What understandings and misunderstandings do the children have about their similarities and differences? What guesses do you have about where the children developed their ideas? Did you pick up on any unintentional biases related to identity?

- How might the curiosity and ease with which the children talk about differences inspire your work as you navigate the complexity of supporting their development?

- How does the children's desire for relationships influence their conversation?

- Observe the children you teach to uncover their ideas about identity. How do they show you they are developing positive self- and family identities? How are they showing you they understand and appreciate differences?

Examine the Environment

- How might the elements of the social and emotional climate and curriculum Nadia describes allow children and adults to feel comfortable having conversations about differences?

Consider Multiple Perspectives

The second edition of *Anti-Bias Education for Young Children and Ourselves* (Derman-Sparks & Edwards with Goins 2020) outlines four core goals of anti-bias education:

- Each child will demonstrate self-awareness, confidence, family pride, and positive social identities.

- Each child will express comfort and joy with human diversity, use accurate language for human differences, and form deep, caring human connections across all dimensions of human diversity.

- Each child will increasingly recognize unfairness (injustice), have language to describe unfairness, and understand that unfairness hurts.

- Each child will demonstrate empowerment and skills to act, with others or alone, against prejudice and/or discriminatory actions.

Consider these goals as you review children's conversations. Where do you see evidence of children demonstrating the goals? What role might a teacher play to support the development of these goals with the children?

I invite families to collaborate and think with the teachers and children. We make a plan about how to best support the children in understanding their identities and the world around them. By having these real and significant talks with young children, we can build an inclusive and respectful school culture that honors differences.

Using the four core goals of anti-bias education (see "Consider Multiple Perspectives" on page 134), I have learned how important it is to be proactive in supporting children in learning about who they are and in having family pride. Classroom conversations about diversity should not be a one-time thing, but ongoing. Each child and family has their own story to tell; in the beginning of the school year, my teaching team and I plan ways to help children and families share their individual and family lives. We engage them in experiences around the anti-bias goals and emphasize that similarities and differences are natural, positive aspects of being human:

- We invite all the families to visit our classroom to share their religious and cultural traditions and celebrations, their family recipes, and their favorite books.

- We use literature as a wonderful way to introduce children to a range of people, to see themselves represented, and to acknowledge that all of us are the same and different in some ways.

- We invite the children to create art pieces to highlight what they know about themselves and to emphasize the anti-bias goal of self-awareness and confidence.

I have learned so much from this group of amazing children. I want to honor their insatiable curiosity and desire for deep relationships with others. I know I must do challenging work to support and advocate for them. As we learn about our similarities and differences, we build a strong foundation of anti-bias education and help make a difference in the world, one conversation at a time!

About the Authors

Nadia Jaboneta is a program coordinator and classroom teacher at Pacific Primary, a preschool in San Francisco, California. She has 21 years of experience teaching young children, training teachers, consulting, and facilitating workshops on various early childhood education topics.

Deb Curtis has spent the past 35 years working with children and teachers in early childhood programs. She developed the Thinking Lens with Margie Carter and Ann Pelo.

Photographs: p. 130, © Getty Images; pp. 132, 133 (both), courtesy of Nadia Jaboneta

Accreditation

This chapter supports the following NAEYC Early Learning Program Accreditation Standards and Topic Areas:

Standard 1: Relationships
1.D Creating a Predictable, Consistent, and Harmonious Classroom

Standard 3: Teaching
3.B Creating Caring Communities for Learning

Pink Power and Bathroom Signs

Exploring Gender and Fairness

Jamie Solomon

"Oh no, the girls are coming! Let's go!" The group of boys quickly left our classroom loft as a few girls ascended the staircase, singing the words to "Let It Go" from the Disney movie *Frozen*. The boys covered their ears as the girls raised their voices. Both the boys and the girls seemed to enjoy this interaction, the energy quickly building.

This chapter is adapted from an article originally published by the North American Reggio Emilia Alliance in its journal, *Innovations in Early Education: The International Reggio Emilia Exchange*, Volume 24.3.

Later on, I watched as a couple of girls pretended to spray a group of boys with "pink power," stretching their arms out in the direction of the boys while making the sound of an aerosol can. The boys yelled in protest, running away to escape the pink power spray. Rather than simply continuing to monitor the situation, I began to ask the children about exclusion and stereotypes: "Is it okay to act like a whole group of people is bad? I notice many boys are acting like they don't like that song. But I know some boys who do."

As the week continued with more games and actions that had a boys-versus-girls dynamic, I determined that the social climate in my classroom of 4-year-olds was problematic. Their play had underlying messages of discrimination and gender bias. I realized that I needed to get involved more intentionally.

The Sneetches Allegory

First, I turned to children's literature to help broach the ideas of segregation and discrimination. Though these topics are complicated, I knew that children are capable of discussing fairness, kindness, and individuality. Using the Dr. Seuss book *The Sneetches*, we read about how part of a group's identity was used to segregate them and determine privilege. In the story, the creatures called Sneetches who have stars on their bellies automatically inherit a more elite status in society than their "plain-belly" counterparts, who are marginalized and considered second-class citizens. Reading the story promptly gave way to a group discussion on fairness: "Like if boys play with only boys and girls play with only girls, then that's not fair," Dusty pointed out. My coteachers and I began to partner boys and girls together for activities, using stories like *The Sneetches* as inspiration.

Building an Understanding of Fairness

In the weeks that followed, we continued to explore discrimination, bias, and fairness through more book read-alouds, discussions, and activities. Our curriculum took an unexpected, exciting new course when one child in the class, Leelah, came to school one day with a different but related concern. Her mother, Nadia, shared a conversation from the night before when she and Leelah went to use the bathroom at a restaurant.

Leelah had paused before entering, looking up at the women's bathroom sign, an image she had probably seen over a hundred times in her life.

Leelah: That's not fair!

Nadia: What's not fair?

Leelah: That has a dress, but you don't wear dresses.

Leelah reasoned that because the image of the female was not representative of her mom, it was an unfair depiction. When asked what she wanted to do about it, Leelah decided, "I'm gonna talk to my friends about it at circle time."

I invited Leelah to raise her concern to the other children at circle time and was surprised by how enthusiastically the children jumped into the conversation, discussing where else they had seen the signs and specifically pointing out why they thought the images were problematic:

Clea: Ms. Nadia doesn't even wear dresses!

Margot: Because boys can wear dresses and girls can have short hair.

My coteachers and I held a series of discussions about this issue over the next several days, asking the children questions and recording their answers and ideas so that we could refer back to them.

What Would Make This Fairer?

Aiden: Maybe it can be a family bathroom.

Kaleb: My family bathroom [at home] doesn't have [pictures].

Clea: How 'bout it's a bathroom for girls *and* boys?

Cade: Sometimes when I'm with my mom and sister, I use the girls' bathroom. . . . It's okay.

Beatrice: How 'bout you can share the bathroom?

Leelah: It'll be more fair if it was just boys wearing dresses.

Ryan: [I saw the sign] going to the airport.

Kaleb: Because the boss doesn't want to change anything.

Sophia: It's fair if you have bathrooms for sisters.

Who Should We Tell About this Problem?

Cade: The person who owns the restaurant.

Dusty: Tell someone who knows about all the potties.

Robby: We can Skype President Obama.

Kaleb: Maybe we can talk to the boss and our parents.

Beatrice: Maybe we can FaceTime with them.

Violet: George Washington's office.

Jack: The boss. Just the boss.

What Should We Tell the "Boss"?

Clea: We should tell them these rules are not fair.

Wheeler: Tell the boss and our parents to change the rule. The boss does a lot of stuff.

Warren: Everybody should tell the boss that's not fair—even the strangers, even the kids next door [at our second site]. We should go on a field trip there across the street. We could yell so loud they can hear us.

Kaleb: Should we ask the boss, "Can we try this?"

Though Leelah initially brought the children's attention to the female pictogram's stereotypical form, her peers started taking issue with the separation of people by gender. We began to examine signs from around the world, comparing them with those in our community. Beatrice pointed out the bold line drawn between the female and male image on a co-ed bathroom sign, describing it as "separating." Other children voiced their agreement and even pointed out that the adult bathroom at our school also had this sign posted on its door. Because the children expressed discontent with the sign, we suggested they design their own bathroom signs.

The children were already discussing and disputing stereotypes ("Not *all* girls have long hair"), but they didn't yet have the word. To help them talk about their ideas, I introduced them to the word *stereotype* one day at circle time. I started by asking the children to list some "girl things." As soon as I started jotting down each child's idea (like "sparkly things"), other children promptly countered the idea with a real-world example ("Our teacher Randy wears sparkly earrings"). The same thing occurred when I asked the children to list "boy things." They quickly saw that they really could not call anything a "girl thing" or a "boy thing."

Taking Action as Active Citizens

Inspired by the children's desire to tell a "boss" about the signage issue, I contacted two parents affiliated with our school who work for the city of San Francisco in the department responsible for public signage. These parents, Christina and Edgar, invited us to city hall for a field trip. A week later, we marched up the steps of city hall as a class, made our way to a conference room, and sat down for a meeting. Christina and Edgar told the children about plans for renovating a nearby playground, which included updates to the public bathroom. We shared our concerns about bathroom sign images and they listened. Though nothing definitive resulted from this meeting, we all came away with the powerful experience of being heard.

At this point, the children all agreed that the adult bathroom signs at our school must change, and Emmy came to school one day with a drawing and a transcription of her ideas that read "No. The boy picture is not fair. Girl picture is not fair. The sign should look different . . . just a picture of a toilet would be fair."

Emmy's idea received unanimous support, and the children decided that it solved our problem. We found a sign featuring a toilet pictogram online and called a meeting with the "bosses" of our school. The children were delighted to get approval from the directors to change the sign, and their excitement doubled when our new sign arrived in the mail.

With a couple of powerful experiences under their belt, the children pushed forward in hopes of making the same change in the bathrooms at our site across the street. At the children's request, my coteacher and I helped them compose a letter to the executive director, Belann Giaretto:

Dear Belann,

"The signs are not even fair at the OSS [Orange Sun School]. Belann, the bathroom signs are not kind because they are separating. We have to all stay together." —Kaleb

"Belann . . . We should buy more signs and give them to people we don't even know and go on field trips. They might not even know about stereotype and we have to teach them." —Dusty

"Belann, we got a bathroom sign for the OSS [Orange Sun School] and we hope you like it! Can we tell the kids that the bathroom signs are unfair? And we need to get them a new sign because we want a sign with a toilet picture and words that say 'all gender' because 'all gender' means all people." —Sophia

"Thank you for letting us give you a letter. We want to change the bathroom signs." —Margot

When we delivered the letter, Belann called the children who were playing in the yard to gather around and listen to our words. Afterward, she led us to the adult bathrooms to replace the old signs with our new ones.

Conclusion

It is our responsibility as educators to engage young children in social justice work. In a society with powerful prevailing stereotypes, children tend to adopt biased notions, just like those before them. Yet when a trusted adult poses questions that challenge the status quo, we see how children use their curiosity and natural inclination toward fairness to explore what's right and how they want to live in the world. Though in many ways our society discourages thinking and caring about injustice (Goss 2012), young children pursue their convictions with fearlessness and fervor, wearing their hearts proudly on their sleeves.

About the Author

Jamie Solomon, MA, is director at Scuola Creativa in Ferndale, MI. She's long taken a special interest in gender identity development in young children and focused her teacher research accordingly.

naeyc®
Accreditation

This chapter supports the following NAEYC Early Learning Program Accreditation Standards and Topic Areas:

Standard 1: Relationships
1.D Creating a Predictable, Consistent, and Harmonious Classroom

Standard 2: Curriculum
2.A Essential Characteristics
2.B Social and Emotional Development

Standard 3: Teaching
3.B Creating Caring Communities for Learning

"What About People Like Me?"

Teaching Preschoolers About Segregation and "Peace Heroes"

Nadia Jaboneta

As part of the anti-bias curriculum at the preschool where I teach, we study the life of Dr. Martin Luther King, Jr. Learning about Dr. King's life provides us with a wonderful opportunity to reflect on the principles he stood for. These are ideas my colleagues and I believe are very appropriate for preschoolers to explore and revisit often.

We focus on Dr. King's desire for all people to be treated fairly regardless of the color of their skin. Solving problems with words; being fair, kind, and inclusive; appreciating similarities and differences among people—these are all ideas we include during morning meetings, small group activities, read-alouds, and regular conversations.

In October 2018, I began by reading a book to the 4- and 5-year-olds in my classroom that was written by a former teacher at our school. Titled *Martin Luther King, Jr. and You*, the book begins by describing Dr. King and his family, his work as a pastor, and his role in the community. One page introduces his work with Rosa Parks and states that the bus company had an unfair rule: "Their rule was that only some people could sit at the front of the bus." The next page then shares how the community boycotted the bus company. The book does not explain segregation.

When I read this part of the book, I noticed that many of the children looked confused. I paused the read-aloud and asked them to share their questions. Elena asked, "Who could sit at the front?" Then Jane wondered, "Why couldn't Rosa Parks sit at the front of the bus?"

I wasn't sure how to respond. I thought to myself, "Is it age appropriate to introduce them to segregation? How would I explain it?" I decided to respond by telling the children, "Our country has had a lot of unfair rules based on the color of people's skin. There used to be a bus rule that said only White people could sit in the front. Black people had to sit in the back. Rosa Parks was a Black woman and she had to sit in the back."

Many of the children looked shocked. Several shouted out, "That's not fair!" and "That's not okay!" One child put her hands over her ears and said, "This is scary. I don't want to hear about it."

Marie, a White child, then announced, "Oh, phew! That wouldn't happen to me. I'm White!" Before I had time to think about how to reply to this statement, Elena, a multiracial child, exclaimed, "What about people like me? Like Sofia? That is not fair! We are your friends!"

I first responded by agreeing with the children that this was not a fair rule. I reminded them that the rule changed because Rosa Parks worked closely with Dr. King and their community to make it better. "They worked together, just like we do in our classroom community," I told them. "If something unfair happens to someone in our community, it is all of our responsibility to help make change. People of all skin colors work together to make things fair." Marie really listened. She then added, "I want to help my friends! I want to help change unfair rules!"

Reflections, Questions, and a Passion for Developing Leaders

As I reflected on our conversation later that day, I felt unsure about what I said and the role I should have played in this discussion. Had I given the children too little information? Too much?

Marie's remark, "Oh, phew! That wouldn't happen to me. I'm White!" really stood out. It reminded me that educators have lots of work to do in helping young children (and many adults) see that just because something may not directly affect us, that does not mean we should not care or should not do something about it.

I also thought about Elena's response. She immediately shared her thoughts, standing up for herself and others as a leader. She helped Marie think about what she was saying and prompted the whole class to understand that working to increase fairness is about all of us and is everyone's responsibility. As her teacher, it was wonderful for me to see her confident self-identity. In a moment in which I hesitated, she was willing to take a risk to speak up about unfairness. She was showing her competence—and she answered my inner question showing that, yes, these are topics children can handle.

Using the Thinking Lens to reflect further on my role with the children, families, and colleagues, I thought about the following:

- **What is my role as the children's teacher?** I would like to learn alongside the children as well as be a leader in helping to guide their critical thinking and problem solving around social justice issues. I want them to be well prepared for their future history and civics classes and, as an essential part of that preparation, I want them to develop their power to make the world better.

Each and Every Child

- **What do children want to know? What do children already know and understand?** Children have questions about what is happening in the world today and about history. I planned to observe, listen, and think deeper with the children about these questions.

- **What is developmentally appropriate and socially and emotionally appropriate for young children?** As I listened to the children's questions, I thought about the best way to answer. How much should children know about past and present injustices? How much background knowledge did I need to provide for them to think meaningfully about social justice issues? Was I telling them enough? Was I going too far? I planned to do research and collaborate with my colleagues and the children's families to agree on what is appropriate for the different age groups.

- **How can I help children feel safe with all the scary things going on in our world?** Often children come to school and share knowledge they have learned at home about our current political climate or about violence in their communities or other places. What is my role when these conversations emerge? How can I help them develop their sense of safety?

- **How can I introduce powerful "Peace Heroes" in a positive way?** An important part of my anti-bias teaching is exposing children to a diverse group of leaders we call Peace Heroes from history and from today. I purposefully select Peace Heroes from around the world, such as Dr. Martin Luther King, Jr., Malala Yousafzai, and Mahatma Gandhi, and also from our community, such as Harvey Milk (California's first openly gay elected official). I know I have to provide context to explain these leaders' accomplishments, but should I include information about the violence that was often a part of these people's stories? If yes, how might I do that?

Asking Big Questions and Developing Powerful Knowledge

After our initial conversation about segregation, we embarked on a 7-month journey learning about important Peace Heroes in our world and what our role could be in making this world a better place. Several weeks in, I realized that our investigation was about so much more. The children had big questions. They wanted to have real conversations and understand why things happen in our world. They asked about life, death, fairness, skin color, and race.

Recently, I was asked by a colleague, "What's your favorite thing about your work with young children?" I answered, "The spontaneous conversations we have about how the world works." As I continue my journey as an anti-bias educator, I think often about what is hard and what is rewarding about this work. Although I love engaging in real conversations with the young children in my classroom, it is challenging. I don't know when these conversations will arise or what children will say or ask. My hope is that I can be as prepared as possible and answer children in a way that is honest, is developmentally appropriate, respects their competence and point of view, helps them feel safe, and shows them their power to change the world.

The rest of the school year, the children, my colleagues, and I thought together about what our roles are and what we can do as Peace Heroes in our communities to make this world a better place. We often sang the song "What Can One Little Person Do?," by Sally Rogers (which is available for free at https://childrensmusic.org/songs/peace/16/what-can-one-little-person-do and includes several Peace Heroes for the children to learn about). The children answered that question with many ideas that give me hope for the future.

People should sit wherever they want on public transportation! I want to help change unfair rules.

If someone is sad, I can give them a hug.

I will protect the people of the world.

I will help get rid of bad guys and make this world a safe place.

I help people. I say, "Do you need help?" and then I help them.

I will plant seeds so people can have healthy food.

Not fight! Use my words. That's what Dr. King did. He didn't use guns. He fought with his words.

About the Author

Nadia Jaboneta is a program coordinator and classroom teacher at Pacific Primary preschool in San Francisco, California. She has 21 years of experience teaching young children, training teachers, consulting, and facilitating workshops on various early childhood education topics.

Photographs: pp. 142, 144, 145, © Getty Images; p. 146, courtesy of the author

naeyc®
Accreditation
™

This chapter supports the following NAEYC Early Learning Program Accreditation Standards and Topic Areas:

Standard 2: Curriculum
2.B Social and Emotional Development
2.L Social Studies

Standard 3: Teaching
3.F Making Learning Meaningful for All Children

Standard 6: Staff Competencies, Preparation, and Support
6.B Professional Identity and Recognition

From Teacher to Equity Activist

Megan Pamela Ruth Madison

Megan Pamela Ruth Madison is an early childhood scholar, activist, and practitioner based in New York City. She holds a master's degree in early childhood education from Dominican University and a bachelor's in studies in religion from the University of Michigan. Currently, she is pursuing her doctorate at Heller School for Social Policy and Management at Brandeis University. Her research examines the impact of "color blind" policymaking on racial inequities in the field of early childhood education. Megan works part-time as a trainer for the Center for Racial Justice in Education, the Human Root, and the New York Early Childhood Professional Development Institute. In this role, she facilitates workshops for teachers and families on race, gender, and sexuality. She recently completed a term as the first student representative on the NAEYC National Governing Board after several years serving as a cofacilitator of the association's Diversity and Equity Interest Forum. Megan also serves on the Board of Directors for Jews for Racial and Economic Justice.

taught me that joy and play and community are possible. They taught me that with a little love, roses can grow even from concrete.

What did the fairness projects look like in your classroom?

While in the classroom, I struggled to find a way to integrate concepts of fairness and social justice into the curriculum. We talked a little about the civil rights movement and environmental justice, but I was unsure of what I was allowed to address and how. I felt scared of making a mistake and unclear about what social justice in the classroom could look like.

What were your early days in early childhood education like? What was your role? What was your classroom like?

I worked with young children as a babysitter in middle school and then in high school in my church's nursery school. So as a college student, working as an assistant in a Waldorf elementary school seemed like the perfect part-time job. After I graduated, I moved to Chicago and became a preschool teacher at the Carole Robertson Center for Learning (CRCL) while working on my master's degree in early childhood education at night. I loved my classroom. I loved the kids and families. I loved my coworkers. CRCL felt like home.

The school was founded with a social justice mission and is firmly rooted in the community. We used a coteaching model, so my favorite thing about my classroom is that I got to work alongside some truly fantastic educators who were generous with their deep knowledge of the community we served. My colleagues were magic makers. They saw the assets that each child and family brought and found everyday ways to highlight those strengths. Even in the most stressful conditions, my colleagues

> I was really committed to fairness in terms of my pedagogical approach and in my relationships with families.

I was really committed to fairness in terms of my pedagogical approach and in my relationships with families. From the ways that we respected children's free play to the ways we developed our classroom rules, I strove to create a classroom environment in which young children had agency over their daily lives. We conducted home visits and implemented a dual language pilot program, trying our hardest to use family engagement strategies that were culturally and linguistically responsive. I understand now that all of that is a part of equitable practices and anti-bias education.

Why did you start thinking about social justice issues in early childhood education?

I went to a social justice curriculum fair and picked up a copy of *Rethinking Early Childhood Education* [by Ann Pelo (2008)].

Each and Every Child

I liked the cover and it was one of the few resources they had for early childhood educators. In it, there's an essay by Charles Bruner where he talks about the low status and compensation of early childhood educators as a social justice issue. It was like a lightbulb went on! I felt like "Yes, this is the problem! It is so hard for us to do what's right on behalf of the children and families we love when we are struggling to make ends meet ourselves." Educators' well-being is connected. We can't get to thriving children and families and communities on the backs of struggling educators. In the words of Robin Wall Kimmerer, "all flourishing is mutual."

That was a pivotal moment for me in starting to understand that these social inequities are systemic in nature, that they have to do with policies and practices beyond any one individual. I remember thinking, there was someone, somewhere, at some level of government who decided that I should be paid $40,000 and my coteacher should only make half of that—even though we had the same job description. It didn't seem fair, and it also didn't seem like it was in the best interest of children and families.

What did learning about anti-bias education mean to you?

Learning about anti-bias education allowed me to bring together my passion for social justice with my love of early childhood curriculum and pedagogy. Before I heard of anti-bias education, I had never seen examples of activism that involved teachers or young children. I thought that being an activist was something that had to happen outside of school hours, in my free time, and I thought, "Well, that's never going to

happen, because as a teacher . . . I have no free time." Anti-bias education allowed me to see my teaching *as* activism.

Can you talk about your progression toward thinking of yourself as an activist and advocate for social justice in early childhood education?

At the end of *Anti-Bias Education for Young Children and Ourselves*, Louise Derman-Sparks and Julie Olsen Edwards (2010) write,

> Ultimately, we cannot fully bring about change in our early childhood programs and in the lives of children and families without improving the economic realities and institutions of the larger society. Anti-bias education work has its own contribution to make, but it is not enough. If we want to see the full vision of anti-bias education come to fruition, then we must work to address a wide range of social and economic justice issues that affect children, their families, and us as their advocates. (159)

This really resonates with me. It's just so clear that if we are to achieve NAEYC's vision of all children thriving and living in a society dedicated to ensuring they reach their full potential, we need to participate in large social change movements, from Black Lives Matter to Close the Camps to Me Too.

I still wrestle with the titles of activist and advocate, in part because I see the work I do as an integral part of my professional responsibilities as an early childhood educator and my spiritual responsibilities as a human being. The NAEYC Code of Ethical Conduct (2016) states that, "above all, we shall not harm children" (8). We know that white supremacy, the patriarchy, heteronormativity,

you do in your spare time." I think of my ancestors and all the people who survived enslavement, Jim Crow, the New Jim Crow . . . the least I can do to honor all that they've given me is to stand firmly in my power and keep bending the arc of justice as far as I possibly can in my lifetime.

What are your thoughts for preschool teachers reading this? What are some doable ways preschool teachers can become activists?

Start by finding a trusted friend or colleague and having an honest conversation with them about what keeps you up at night. Talk to them about what's in your heart, what your struggles are, and what your passions are. Sometimes talking it out with another person can really help us clarify what we care about and why. Once you're a little bit clearer on that, you'll be ready to find and join a group of other people who care about that same issue.

ableism, settler colonialism, the gender binary, and any other system that inequitably distributes power, resources, and privilege to one group at the expense of another harms children. *All* children. We therefore have an ethical responsibility to play our part in dismantling these systems.

There's a Jewish teaching that often grounds me in this work: "You are not obligated to complete the work, and neither are you free to desist from it." To me, that means it's not up to me alone, in one day or one school year or even one lifetime, to end oppression. But I am responsible to join together with others—past, present, and future—and do my part.

Marian Wright Edelman taught us that "service is the rent we pay for being. It is the very purpose of life, and not something

> There's a big myth out there that change happens when one person, all by herself, stands up for what's right.

There's a big myth out there that change happens when one person, all by herself, stands up for what's right. Usually when that happens, that one person gets fired. All social change happens when groups of people organize together to issue a demand in a collective voice. The good news is that it isn't hard to find other changemakers these days. We're living in a movement moment. If you look, I'm pretty sure you can find your people. They're out there, waiting for you to bring your unique story, gifts, and energy to the movement.

What do you want early childhood teachers to pay attention to when they look at NAEYC's position statement on equity?

Pay attention to your feelings as you read through it. What surprises you? Scares you? Excites you? What makes you angry? What makes you sad? The beautiful thing about emotions is that they are all right! There's no such thing as a wrong feeling. And every emotion is sending us a message about ourselves, where we are, and what we need. Once we know what we need, that can help us figure out our next step.

Do you have any final thoughts you'd like to share?

There is no such thing as neutral or apolitical teaching. Every choice we make in the classroom either reinforces or resists existing systems of privilege, power, and oppression in our society: who we call on during circle time, what read-alouds we choose, how we greet a family member. That reality can feel overwhelming, but I think it can also feel empowering. It means that every single day, we have thousands of opportunities to make our society fairer, safer, more sustainable, and more loving. It means that the work we do really matters.

> Every choice we make in the classroom either reinforces or resists existing systems of privilege, power, and oppression in our society: who we call on during circle time, what read-alouds we choose, how we greet a family member. That reality can feel overwhelming, but I think it can also feel empowering.

Whoever is reading this, I hope you know that you are not alone in this work. You are a part of a larger movement of educators, caregivers, and young people all working together to build a world rooted in racial, economic, and social justice. From the bottom of my heart, thank you for the work you do every single day. It really matters.

Photographs: pp. 150, 152, courtesy of the author

Accreditation

This chapter supports the following NAEYC Early Learning Program Accreditation Standards and Topic Areas:

Standard 1: Relationships
1.D Creating a Predictable, Consistent, and Harmonious Classroom

Standard 2: Curriculum
2.B Social and Emotional Development

Standard 6: Staff Competencies, Preparation, and Support
6.A Supportive Work Environment

Standard 8: Community Relationships
8.C Acting as a Citizen in the Neighborhood and the Early Childhood Community

References

Barbarin, O., & G.M. Crawford. 2006. "Acknowledging and Reducing Stigmatization of African American Boys." *Young Children* 61 (6): 79–86.

Bian L., S.J. Leslie, & A. Cimpian. 2017. "Gender Stereotypes About Intellectual Ability Emerge Early and Influence Children's Interests." *Science* 355 (6323): 389–91. doi:10.1126/scienceaah6524.

Brown, C.S., H. Ali, E.A. Stone, & J.A. Jewell. 2017. "US Children's Stereotypes and Prejudicial Attitudes Toward Arab Muslims." *Analyses of Social Issues and Public Policy* 17 (1): 60–83. doi:10.1111/asap.12129.

Derman-Sparks, L., & J.O. Edwards. With C.M. Goins. 2020. *Anti-Bias Education for Young Children and Ourselves.* 2nd ed. Washington, DC: NAEYC.

Derman-Sparks, L., & J.O. Edwards. 2010. *Anti-Bias Education for Young Children and Ourselves.* Washington, DC: NAEYC.

EDC (Education Development Center). 2019a. *Games for Young Mathematicians.* www.ym.edc.org.

EDC. 2019b. *Supporting Emergent Bilingual Children in Early Learning: Promising Practices and Checklist.* Report. Waltham, MA: EDC. www.edc.org/sites/default/files/uploads/Supporting-Emergent-Bilingual-Children_English.pdf.

Ferguson, R.F., & T. Robertson. 2019. *The Formula: Unlocking the Secrets to Raising Highly Successful Children.* Dallas, TX: BenBella Books.

Goss, E. 2012. "If I Were President: Teaching Social Justice in the Primary Classroom." In *Our Inquiry, Our Practice: Undertaking, Supporting, and Learning from Early Childhood Teacher Research(ers),* eds. G. Perry, B. Henderson, & D.R. Meier, 77–92. Washington, DC: NAEYC.

Hassinger-Das, B., K. Hirsh-Pasek, & R.M. Golinkoff. 2017. "The Case of Brain Science and Guided Play: A Developing Story." *Young Children* 72 (2): 45–50.

KIDS COUNT. 2018. "The Number of Bilingual Kids in America Continues to Rise." KIDS COUNT Data Center, January 11. https://datacenter.kidscount.org/updates/show/184-the-number-of-bilingual-kids-in-america-continues-to-rise.

Kirwan Institute (Kirwan Institute for the Study of Race and Ethnicity). 2015. *Understanding Implicit Bias.* http://kirwaninstitute.osu.edu/research/understanding-implicit-bias.

NAEYC. 2016. *Code of Ethical Conduct and Statement of Commitment.* Brochure. Rev. ed. Washington, DC: NAEYC.

NAEYC. 2019. "Advancing Equity in Early Childhood Education." Position statement. Washington, DC: NAEYC. www.naeyc.org/sites/default/files/globally-shared/downloads/PDFs/resources/position-statements/naeycadvancingequitypositionstatement.pdf.

Nemeth, K.N. 2012. *Basics of Supporting Dual Language Learners: An Introduction for Educators of Children from Birth through Age 8.* Washington, DC: NAEYC.

OCR (US Department of Education Office for Civil Rights). 2014. "Data Snapshot: School Discipline." Civil Rights Data Collection. https://ocrdata.ed.gov/Downloads/CRDC-School-Discipline-Snapshot.pdf.

OWH (US Department of Health and Human Services Office on Women's Health). 2019. "Body Image." Last modified March 27. www.womenshealth.gov/mental-health/body-image-and-mental-health/body-image.

Price, C.L., & E.A. Steed. 2016. "Culturally Responsive Strategies to Support Young Children with Challenging Behavior." *Young Children* 71 (5): 36–43.

Strasser, J., & L.M. Bresson. 2017. *Big Questions for Young Minds: Extending Children's Thinking.* Washington, DC: NAEYC.

Wanless, S.B., & P.A. Crawford. 2016. "Reading Your Way to a Culturally Responsive Classroom." *Young Children* 71 (2): 8–15.

Yates, T.M., & A.K. Marcelo. 2014. "Through Race-Colored Glasses: Preschoolers' Pretend Play and Teachers' Ratings of Preschooler Adjustment." *Early Childhood Research Quarterly* 29 (1): 1–11. doi:10.1016/j.ecresq.2013.09.003.

Zeigler, K., & S.A. Camarota. 2018. "Almost Half Speak a Foreign Language in America's Largest Cities." Center for Immigration Studies, September 19. https://cis.org/Report/Almost-Half-Speak-Foreign-Language-Americas-Largest-Cities.

About the Editors

Susan Friedman is senior director of publishing and professional learning at the National Association for the Education of Young Children (NAEYC). In this role, she leads the content development work of NAEYC's books, periodicals, digital content, and professional learning teams. Early childhood educators rely on NAEYC's award-winning content to stay current on research and best practices they can implement in their classrooms. Susan has extensive prior experience in content programming as well as editorial oversight and production with many years of experience creating content on play, developmentally appropriate uses of media, and other topics for educators and families. She has presented at numerous educational conferences, including NAEYC's Professional Learning Institute and Annual Conference, the South by Southwest Education (SXSW EDU) Conference & Festival, and the School Superintendents Association's Early Learning Cohort. Susan began her career as a preschool teacher at City and Country School in New York City. She holds degrees from Vassar College and the Harvard Graduate School of Education.

Alissa Mwenelupembe has worked in the field of early childhood education for over 18 years as a teacher, coach, director, and college instructor. She serves on the NAEYC National Governing Board. Alissa holds a bachelor's degree from the University of Southern Indiana and a master's degree in early childhood education from Ball State University, and she is currently pursuing a doctorate in early childhood education at Ball State University. As a Black woman working in early childhood education and navigating higher education spheres, she is well versed in the issues of equity and diversity. Her research interests center around the social and emotional development of children of color, primarily those living in families and communities that are not a racial match. Alissa has presented both locally and nationally at early childhood conferences, including NAEYC's Professional Learning Institute and Annual Conference, the Maryland Head Start Association Conference, and the Indiana Association for the Education of Young Children's Annual Conference.

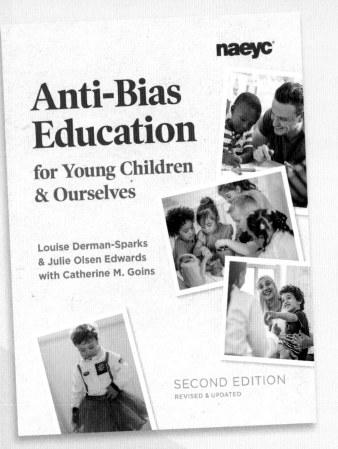

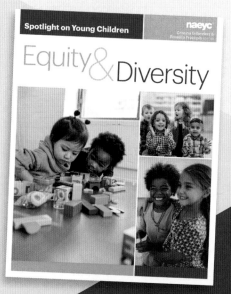